I0813626

Knitting THE U.S.A.

Knitting THE U.S.A.

50 Easy-to-Follow Designs for Beautiful Beanies Inspired by Each State in America

Nancy Bates

weldonowen

To my wonderful siblings,

Linda, Rick, Susan, Yvonne, Yvette, Brenda, Joe, and Kim.
We may be as different as the fifty states, but
I couldn't imagine a world without you.

CONTENTS

INTRODUCTION

Designing hats to represent each of the fifty US states was an exciting yet daunting challenge at first. Where to start? As a Californian, I'm very familiar with the West Coast states, but my exposure to the East Coast had consisted of one- to two-week vacations every few years. I hadn't even been to most of the South or the Midwest. Yet I instinctively knew each state had something that made it unique. But what was it? How is Nebraska different from Kansas or Maryland different from Connecticut? Does Ohio have mountains? What color is the Mississippi River? I had so many questions! But with *lots* of research and by connecting with the people who live there, I found my answers—and so much more. The creative and joyful process of bringing the states to life through knitting could begin! The hardest part became choosing just one design for each state.

I've often pictured the entire United States as one giant neighborhood and each state as a different home with a different family. Like most neighborhoods, one family might play music that's unfamiliar to you or speak with an accent while another might cook food you can't name but that smells delicious. Even the homes are usually different sizes and styles with incredibly different landscaping. In short, each place has something about it that makes it unique. It could be the way an old tree beautifies the neighborhood or how the entire home just exudes a peaceful calm. Maybe it's the way it always smells like someone is baking or how the people who live there cheerfully say hello when you pass by. The uniqueness isn't always obvious at first, but it's there. One simply needs to look, listen, and step out of the front door. The same is true of discovering and appreciating the uniqueness of each of the fifty states.

As you knit, purl, cable, bobble, and duplicate stitch your way through the pages of this book, I hope that you, too, discover at least one thing about each state. Who knows, you just might be inspired to search for wild sego lilies in Utah (page 211), explore caves in Missouri (page 137), taste Frogmore stew in South Carolina (page 95), or witness the great sandhill crane migration in Nebraska (page 141). Whatever you discover, I hope it's something new to you. After all, you might not see squirrels in Hawaii, oceans in Oklahoma, or manatees in Alaska. But visit your amazing neighbors and you can see all those things!

See you around the neighborhood—with my knitting in hand, of course!

THE BASICS

Choosing Yarn

All of the designs in this book (with the exception of one color in Alaska) call for worsted weight yarn (also referred to as a #4). Worsted weight is warm and cozy, making it a great choice for hats. It's also quick and easy to work with (especially when trying new stitches) and doesn't require a lot of yardage per hat. Because superwash merino is durable and washable and has amazing depth of color, I lean toward using it for most designs. Other wools, wool blends, and acrylics are good choices, too. Cotton is not recommended because of its lack of memory—the hat will not keep its shape. Just be sure your choice feels great and has good stitch definition so that all that stitchwork isn't lost in the yarn. Now that you know what weight of yarn to choose, it's time for the fun part—color!

To me, choosing colors is by far the most exciting part of starting a new project. You get to decide whether you want your hat to look just like mine or something a little different. The color choices are endless, and personalizing your project is very rewarding. By changing colors, you can turn night into day in California or Delaware. You can turn spring into fall (or vice versa) in Virginia, New York, Arkansas, or Pennsylvania. Do you prefer pink magnolias in Mississippi? Change them up! And those cute boots from Texas can be whatever color your heart desires! Raid your stash. Try something new. It's all up to you. If you're familiar with my books *Knitting the National Parks* and *Knitting California*, you might recognize some of the same yarns and colors used here along with many new ones. Like most knitters, I have my favorites but love trying something new. You'll also find many colors used in more than one design, which helps with stretching that yarn budget.

Gauge and Sizing

Achieving the correct gauge (number of stitches per 1 in. / 2.5 cm) in your knitting is very important in making sure your hat fits. If you knit too tightly, your hat will be small. Too loosely, and it will be large. The hats in this book are designed to be "one size fits most adults." They will fit if you have the correct gauge. Before beginning your chosen design, knit a small swatch (about 4 in. / 10 cm square) in stockinette stitch (or other stitch as specified in the pattern) with the same yarn and same needle you plan to use for the hat. You can also use a "gauge in the round" method if you prefer. Block the swatch, let dry, and then carefully count your stitches against a ruler. Adjust your needles as needed until you get the correct gauge. If you want your hat to fit bigger or smaller, simply go up or down one or two needle sizes to achieve the desired fit. You can also make your hat a bit "slouchier" by adding rows or a bit shorter by removing rows. This takes some thought and planning to be sure your addition or subtraction of rows doesn't interfere with the design. When possible, make these optional changes in areas such as plain stockinette stitch sections.

Casting On

When choosing a cast-on method, be sure to use one that is stretchy and suitable for hats. The long-tail cast-on is my preferred method and the one I use throughout this book. It's consistent, simple, neat, and flexible. If you want to experiment with another method, test a sample ribbing first to check for flexibility before continuing with your hat.

A Note About Duplicate Stitching

In the stranded colorwork of my designs, I never use more than two colors at once. This keeps the projects much more attainable for the majority of knitters, even those just starting out. For many knitters, adding just one more color in a single row makes the project exponentially more difficult. When more than two colors per row are needed to make a design work, I use slip stitches whenever possible. But this technique isn't always enough. This is where duplicate stitching comes in. Duplicate stitching is simple, relaxing, and allows the knitter to add any color anywhere on the design. It takes practice and time, but it's so worth it.

In some, but not all, of my designs, I suggest which color to knit under the

duplicate stitch. My basic rule is, of the two colors you're using in that row, knit with whichever color would offend you least if it peeked out a little behind the duplicate stitch.

You will find instructions for duplicate stitching in the Techniques Glossary (page 224), but I highly recommend watching an online tutorial. Seeing it in action is easier to follow.

Of course, if you are comfortable knitting with three or four colors in one row, by all means, go for it. Simply ignore the "D" symbols and knit in the colors shown.

Wet blocking

Wet blocking is a technique used to give knitted items a neater, finished appearance. I always say, "Wet blocking is to knitting what ironing is to sewing." It's especially important in stranded colorwork because it helps relax the stitches and even out the tension. It also rounds out the top of a hat to reduce any unwanted pointiness. It can even help a hat that's slightly too tight fit a little better.

1. Begin by soaking the hat in a small tub or bowl of cool water. Add a little no-rinse wool wash to the water if desired. If you're concerned about color transfer between dark and light colors, add a commercial "color-catching" sheet to the water. Attach the ribbing end of the hat to the side of the tub using a large clip, keeping the ribbing just above the water level while the rest of the hat soaks. Leaving the ribbing above the waterline keeps it from stretching out too much. Soak the hat for a few minutes.
2. Carefully lift the hat from the water, supporting it from the bottom to avoid excess stretching. Keep the ribbing toward the top to keep it dry, then gently squeeze out as much water as possible from the hat. Do not wring or twist.
3. Roll the hat in a clean, dry towel and gently but firmly press down on the towel to remove excess water.
4. Carefully placing your hat over a bowl or other rounded object (even a balloon) to dry allows for better shaping as opposed to letting it dry flat. Be sure the object is the size you want your finished hat to be. Smooth out any uneven stitches and very gently pull or stretch the hat as needed to remove puckers or make the hat a little bigger. Pat down and shape the crown of the hat, removing any unwanted pointiness. Allow the hat to dry overnight.

THE NORTH

Connecticut

Delaware

Maine

Maryland

Massachusetts

New Hampshire

New Jersey

New York

Pennsylvania

Rhode Island

Vermont

As one of the states of New England, Connecticut features amazing fall foliage, quaint villages, rolling hills, and historic buildings, as well as a strong Native American influence, especially in the names of locations. Connecticut proudly played a key role in the American Revolution earning the nickname "the provision state" at the time. This diverse state is also the birthplace of author Harriet Beecher Stowe, a land of inventions (the Frisbee, pay phones, Polaroid, and submarines) and the place where Mark Twain wrote some of his best work, including *A Connecticut Yankee in King Arthur's Court*. Because of its long coastline and strong ties to the sea, Connecticut was also a leader in wooden shipbuilding for almost three hundred years. This history is still remembered and honored today at the Mystic Seaport Museum, the largest maritime museum in the country.

In this design, a wooden sailing ship glides past a coastline of fall foliage. The twisted knit stitches of the water give the illusion of ripples. Rigging is added using simple embroidery.

SIZE

One size fits an average adult size head (approx. 19 in. / 48 cm – 22 in. / 56 cm)

Finished Circumference: approx. 20¼ in. / 51.5 cm.

YARN

Worsted weight yarn (#4) in seven colors. Shown in:

- **A:** Malabrigo Rios: Denim (25 g / 53 yd. / 48 m)
- **B:** Malabrigo Rios: Black (10 g / 21 yd. / 19 m)
- **C:** Aly Bee Workshop Merino Worsted: Campfire (10 g / 21 yd. / 19 m)
- **D:** *Stunning String Studio Legacy Worsted: Shadow (approx. 8 yd. / 7 m)
- **E:** Malabrigo Rios: Natural (15 g / 32 yd. / 29 m)
- **F:** Malabrigo Rios: Aquamarine (25 g / 53 yd. / 48 m)
- **G:** Stunning String Studio Legacy Worsted: Dove (10 g / 21 yd. / 19 m)

*Used only in duplicate stitching

Optional: 6–8 yd. / 5–7 m of any tan or light brown yarn for the rigging.

Continued on next page

NEEDLES

- US size 5 / 3.75 mm, 16 in. / 40 cm circular knitting needles
- US size 7 / 4.5 mm, 16 in. / 40 cm circular knitting needles
- US size 7 / 4.5 mm, set of double-pointed needles (DPNs)
- (or size needed to obtain gauge)

NOTIONS

3 stitch markers (two of one color and one of another color)

Tapestry needle for weaving in ends and working duplicate stitches and embroidery

GAUGE

With larger needles, approx. 9½ stitches = 2 in. / 5 cm in stranded stockinette stitch, blocked.

Note: If you already know you are a tight knitter (or just want a larger hat), go up one or two needle sizes for both the ribbing and the body of the hat.

With smaller circular needles and color A, cast on 96 stitches. Place single color marker and join in the round being careful not to twist stitches.

Work (k1 tbl, p1) rib pattern for approximately 1½ to 2 in. / 4 to 5 cm.
(tbl=through back loop)

Switch to larger needles and work chart from right to left beginning on Row 1, bottom right corner. Chart repeats three times around the hat.

Use remaining two stitch markers of another color to mark chart repeats.

Note: In order to avoid long "floats" (strands of yarn on the inside of the hat) and to help maintain your tension, do not carry a color more than three or four stitches without twisting the colors around each other in the back of work.

Switch to DPNs when work becomes too small for circular needles.

FINISHING

After chart is complete, cut yarn leaving a 10 in. / 25.5 cm tail. Using a tapestry needle, weave tail through remaining stitches and pull tightly to close circle. Pull tail to inside and weave in all ends.

Block as desired. See page 13 for my favorite hat blocking technique.

After all blocking is complete, work duplicate stitches in colors and locations shown. Using long straight stitches tacked down with tiny straight stitches, add the bowsprit using color D and optional rigging using any tan or light brown yarn. I separated the plies of a worsted weight and used only 2 plies to keep the rigging from looking too thick. See photo for inspiration.

KEY

- K-tbl: Knit through back loop
- K: Knit
- D — Dup: Work duplicate stitches after all knitting and blocking is complete.
- S1: Slip one purlwise with yarn in back.
- K2tog: Knit 2 together
- No Stitch: The "no stitch" squares represent the stitches that were lost due to decreases earlier in the round. *Do not skip a stitch.* Simply treat these squares as if they do not exist.

The image of log cabins has become synonymous with American pioneer life—so much so that they seem like an American invention. However, log cabins were first introduced by Scandinavian settlers in Delaware in the 1600s. The durability and relative simplicity of log homes soon made them a poplular choice for settlers and pioneers across the country. Built with logs and mud using only hand tools, several log cabins from the 1600s and 1700s are still standing today! Wow! Log home construction has come a long way since then, but the warmth, durability, and inherently outdoorsy vibe of log homes and lodges never go out of style.

In the warm colors of a Delaware forest at dusk, this design features a simple log cabin surrounded by a few optional fireflies.

SIZE

One size fits an average adult size head (approx. 19 in. / 48 cm – 22 in. / 56 cm)

Finished Circumference: approx. 20¼ in. / 51.5 cm.

YARN

Worsted weight yarn (#4) in six colors. Shown in:

- **A:** Stunning String Legacy Worsted: Acorn (20 g / 43 yd. / 39 m)
- **B:** Aly Bee Workshop Merino Worsted: Semisweet (15 g / 32 yd. / 29 m)
- **C:** Stunning String Legacy Worsted: Vineyard (10 g / 21 yd. / 19 m)
- **D:** *Stunning String Legacy Worsted: Dried Hops (5 g / 10 yd. / 9 m)
- **E:** Malabrigo Rios: VAA (25 g / 53 yd. / 48 m)
- **F:** Polka Dot Sheep Whitefish Worsted: Slate (20 g / 43 yd. / 39 m)

*Used only in duplicate stitching

Optional: Approx. 5–8 yd. / 4–7 m of Glow in the Dark yarn to make the fireflies. I used Amigurumi Glow in the Dark by Circulo #10.

Continued on next page

NEEDLES

- US size 5 / 3.75 mm, 16 in. / 40 cm circular knitting needles
- US size 7 / 4.5 mm, 16 in. / 40 cm circular knitting needles
- US size 7 / 4.5 mm, set of double-pointed needles (DPNs)
- (or size needed to obtain gauge)

NOTIONS

3 stitch markers (two of one color and one of another color)

Tapestry needle for weaving in ends and working duplicate stitches and embroidery

GAUGE

With larger needles, approx. 9½ stitches = 2 in. / 5 cm in stranded stockinette stitch, blocked.

Note: If you already know you are a tight knitter (or just want a larger hat), go up one or two needle sizes for both the ribbing and the body of the hat.

With smaller circular needles and color A, cast on 96 stitches. Place single color marker and join in the round, being careful not to twist stitches.

Work (k2, p2) rib pattern for approximately 1½ to 2 in. / 4 to 5 cm.

Switch to larger needles and work chart from right to left beginning on Row 1, bottom right corner. Chart repeats three times around the hat. Use remaining two stitch markers of another color to mark chart repeats.

Note: In order to avoid long "floats" (strands of yarn on the inside of the hat) and to help maintain your tension, do not carry a color more than three or four stitches without twisting the colors around each other in the back of work.

Switch to DPNs when work becomes too small for circular needles.

FINISHING

After chart is complete, cut yarn leaving a 10 in. / 25.5 cm tail. Using a tapestry needle, weave tail through remaining stitches and pull tightly to close circle. Pull tail to inside and weave in all ends.

Block as desired. See page 13 for my favorite hat blocking technique.

Optional: After all blocking is complete, use Glow in the Dark Yarn to add fireflies to the forest. To add variety, I used French knots with 2 *or* 4 plies of yarn as well as a few using tiny straight stitches. Add as many or as few as you'd like. See photo for inspiration.

KEY

- ☐ K — Knit
- D Dup — Work duplicate stitches after all knitting and blocking is complete.
- V S1 — Slip one purlwise with yarn in back
- K-tbl — Knit through back loop
- / K2tog — Knit 2 together
- ■ No Stitch — The "no stitch" squares represent the stitches that were lost due to decreases earlier in the round. *Do not skip a stitch.* Simply treat these squares as if they do not exist.

Rugged coastlines, fisheries, lobsters, lighthouses, stormy weather, and charming coastal towns. If these are the images that come to mind when you think about Maine, you wouldn't be wrong. With 3,500 miles of coastline dotted with bays and coves and flanked by thousands of coastal islands, Maine has a strong connection to the sea that dates back to the first humans who lived there. Beyond the coastline, Maine is also a top producer of blueberries, home to an exceptionally large population of moose, and boasts thousands of lakes and ponds. As the easternmost state in the country, it's the first place to see the sunrise in the United States. Maine also rivals any of the New England states when it comes to fall colors. If you find yourself in this history-filled state, don't forget to try Moxie, the unique soda created in 1885 that is now the official state soft drink of Maine.

This design features a rocky coastline and a simplified interpretation of Portland Head Light, the oldest and probably most famous of the sixty-five lighthouses still standing along the coast of Maine.

SIZE

One size fits an average adult size head (approx. 19 in. / 48 cm – 22 in. / 56 cm)

Finished Circumference: approx. 20¼ in. / 51.5 cm.

YARN

Worsted weight yarn (#4) in five colors. Shown in:

- **A:** Ewe 2 Yarn Mellow Worsted: Cliffside (25 g / 54 yd. / 49 m)
- **B:** Polka Dot Sheep Whitefish Worsted: Moose Meadow (10 g / 22 yd. / 20 m)
- **C:** Malabrigo Rios: Denim (10 g / 21 yd. / 19 m)
- **D:** Dragonfly Fibers and Canon Hand Dyes Sylph Worsted: Cloudy Sky (33 g/ 71 yd./ 65 m)
- **E:** Aly Bee Workshop Merino Worsted: Rainy Day (10 g / 21 yd. / 19 m)

For each duplicate stitched lighthouse, you will need approx. 2–3 yd. / 1.75–2.75 m each of natural or white, black, and your chosen color for the roof. I used Aly Bee Workshop Merino Worsted in Farmhouse for the roof. Optional flowers will need the same amount of another color.

Continued on next page

NEEDLES

- US size 5 / 3.75 mm, 16 in. / 40 cm circular knitting needles
- US size 7 / 4.5 mm, 16 in. / 40 cm circular knitting needles
- US size 7 / 4.5 mm, set of double-pointed needles (DPNs)
- (or size needed to obtain gauge)

NOTIONS

3 stitch markers (two of one color and one of another color)

Tapestry needle for weaving in ends and working duplicate stitches and embroidery

GAUGE

With larger needles, approx. 9½ stitches = 2 in. / 5 cm in stranded stockinette stitch blocked.

Note: If you already know you are a tight knitter (or just want a larger hat), go up one or two needle sizes for both the ribbing and the body of the hat.

With smaller circular needles and color A, cast on 96 stitches. Place single color marker and join in the round, being careful not to twist stitches.

Work (k1, p1) rib pattern for approximately 1½ to 2 in. / 4 to 5 cm.

Switch to larger needles and work chart from right to left beginning on Row 1, bottom right corner. Chart repeats three times around the hat. Use remaining two stitch markers of another color to mark chart repeats.

Note: In order to avoid long "floats" (strands of yarn on the inside of the hat) and to help maintain your tension, do not carry a color more than three or four stitches without twisting the colors around each other in the back of work.

Switch to DPNs when work becomes too small for circular needles.

FINISHING

After chart is complete, cut yarn, leaving a 10 in. / 25.5 cm tail. Using a tapestry needle, weave tail through remaining stitches and pull tightly to close circle. Pull tail to inside and weave in all ends.

Block as desired. See page 13 for my favorite hat blocking technique.See photo for inspiration.

Lighthouse(s) and Flowers: After all knitting and blocking is complete, use a tapestry needle and duplicate stitches to add lighthouse(s) where shown on chart. On the black sections of the lighthouse, I added some horizontal straight stitches to help define the shape. I also added one vertical straight stitch for the pole on top of the structure as well as a line between the lighthouse and the building. See photo for inspiration. You can choose to add one lighthouse as I did, or place one lighthouse on each of the outcroppings along the shore. You can make them all the same or make different designs using actual lighthouses as inspiration.

Optional: Using your preferred color, add a few flowers using French knots.

KEY

- ☐ **K** — Knit
- ● **Mb** — Make Bobble: knit in front and back of next stitch 2 times, then lift 2nd, 3rd, and 4th stitches over first stitch and off needle, one at a time
- V **S1** — Slip one purlwise with yarn in back
- D **Dup** — Work duplicate stitches after all knitting and blocking is complete.
- / **K2tog** — Knit 2 together
- ■ **No Stitch** — The "no stitch" squares represent the stitches that were lost due to decreases earlier in the round. *Do not skip a stitch*. Simply treat these squares as if they do not exist.

Note: The entire lighthouse is added using duplicate stitching and a few straight stitches after all knitting and blocking is complete.

A summer spent in Maryland means a summer spent relaxing on beaches, visiting historic sites, strolling along boardwalks, camping and hiking in nature, sailing in the ocean, exploring spectacular museums, and most likely indulging in something tasty seasoned with Old Bay. From the shores of Assateague Island in the east to the forests and farmlands in the west, and all the history and adventure in between, there's no shortage of interesting and exciting things to see and do at *any* time of year. But with a summer visit, one delightful activity is almost certain: at least one sighting of the state bird and state flower!

With the bright colors of summer itself, this design features a patch of wild black-eyed Susans followed by a band of duplicate-stitched orioles nestled between more flowers.

SIZE

One size fits an average adult size head (approx. 19 in. / 48 cm – 22 in. / 56 cm)

Finished Circumference: approx. 20¼ in. / 51.5 cm.

YARN

Worsted weight yarn (#4) in five colors. Shown in:

- **A:** Stunning String Legacy Worsted: Dew Drops (40 g / 86 yd. / 79 m)
- **B:** Aly Bee Workshop Merino Worsted: Fresh Cut (20 g / 40 yd. / 37 m)
- **C:** Stunning String Legacy Worsted: Goldenrod (33 g / 71 yd. / 65 m)
- **D:** *Stunning String Legacy Worsted: Black (5 g / 10 yd. / 9 m)
- **E:** *Stunning String Legacy Worsted: *Calendula (5 g / 10 yd. / 9 m)

*Used only in duplicate stitching

8–10 yd. / 7-9 m of a dark brown yarn to add clusters of French knots for flower centers. I used Malabrigo Rios in Coco. See photo for inspiration.

Continued on next page

NEEDLES

- US size 5 / 3.75 mm, 16 in. / 40 cm circular knitting needles
- US size 7 / 4.5 mm, 16 in. / 40 cm circular knitting needles
- US size 7 / 4.5 mm, set of double-pointed needles (DPNs)
- (or size needed to obtain gauge)

NOTIONS

3 stitch markers (two of one color and one of another color)

Tapestry needle for weaving in ends and working duplicate stitches and embroidery

GAUGE

With larger needles, approx. 9½ stitches = 2 in. / 5 cm in stranded stockinette stitch, blocked.

Note: If you already know you are a tight knitter (or just want a larger hat), go up one or two needle sizes for both the ribbing and the body of the hat.

With smaller circular needles and color A, cast on 96 stitches. Place single color marker and join in the round, being careful not to twist stitches.

Work (k2, p2) rib pattern for approximately 1½ to 2 in. / 4 to 5 cm.

Switch to larger needles and work chart from right to left beginning on Row 1, bottom right corner. Chart repeats three times around the hat. Use remaining two stitch markers of another color to mark chart repeats.

Note: In order to avoid long "floats" (strands of yarn on the inside of the hat) and to help maintain your tension, do not carry a color more than three or four stitches without twisting the colors around each other in the back of work.

Switch to DPNs when work becomes too small for circular needles.

FINISHING

After chart is complete, cut yarn leaving a 10 in. / 25.5 cm tail. Using a tapestry needle, weave tail through remaining stitches and pull tightly to close circle. Pull tail to inside and weave in all ends.

Block as desired. See page 13 for my favorite hat blocking technique.

After blocking is complete, work all duplicate stitches in colors and locations shown using tapestry needle.

Embroidery: Using simple straight stitches and color D, add beaks and feet to the birds. Using the dark brown, add centers to the flowers with clusters of French knots. See photo for inspiration. Optional: Assorted sizes of dark brown buttons can also be used for the centers of the flowers in place of French knots.

KEY

☐ **K**
Knit

[D] **Dup**
Work duplicate stitches after all knitting and blocking is complete.

[/] **K2tog**
Knit 2 together

■ **No Stitch**
The "no stitch" squares represent the stitches that were lost due to decreases earlier in the round. *Do not skip a stitch*. Simply treat these squares as if they do not exist.

From Williamstown to Boston and everywhere in between, brick structures are a common sight throughout Massachusetts. From town halls and universities to everyday homes and businesses, bricks have been a top building material of choice dating back to colonial times. You'll even find them lining the streets in parts of Salem and Boston. Because bricks withstand the ravages of fire, structures made of brick historically last much longer than wooden structures, with one of the oldest brick houses in the state dating back to 1680. Brick is not only durable, it also exudes a historical presence that is felt throughout the state. In Massachusetts, history is so intertwined with modern life that you can enjoy lobster rolls, clam chowder, or Boston cream pie in the same building where patriots once met to plan the American Revolution.

In this design, simple stitches and just-right colors turn your hat into a classic brick building with a slate roof. Optional lantern-shaped charms add an extra historical touch while French knot flowers add a bit of spring or summer color.

SIZE

One size fits an average adult size head (approx. 19 in. / 48 cm – 22 in. / 56 cm)

Finished Circumference: approx. 20¼ in. / 51.5 cm.

YARN

Worsted weight yarn (#4) in five colors. Shown in:

A: Not shown on chart - Malabrigo Rios: Taurus (20 g / 42 yd./ 38 m)

B: Stunning String Legacy Worsted: Stone (25 g / 54 yd. / 49 m)

C: *Malabrigo Rios: Natural (25 g / 53 yd. / 48 m)

D: Peekaboo Yarns Merino Worsted: Yam (25 g / 54 yd. / 49 m)

E: Stunning String Legacy Worsted: Summit Blue (15 g / 32 yd. / 29 m)

*Used only in duplicate stitching

Optional: 4–5 yd. / 3–4 m of any color yarn for the flowers at the base of the building.

Two or more lantern-shaped charms to decorate around the door or in the windows.

Continued on next page

NEEDLES

- US size 5 / 3.75 mm, 16 in. / 40 cm circular knitting needles
- US size 7 / 4.5 mm, 16 in. / 40 cm circular knitting needles
- US size 7 / 4.5 mm, set of double-pointed needles (DPNs)
- (or size needed to obtain gauge)

NOTIONS

3 stitch markers (two of one color and one of another color)

Tapestry needle for weaving in ends and working duplicate stitches and embroidery

GAUGE

With larger needles, approx. 9½ stitches = 2 in. / 5 cm in stranded stockinette stitch, blocked.

Note: If you already know you are a tight knitter (or just want a larger hat), go up one or two needle sizes for both the ribbing and the body of the hat.

With smaller circular needles and color A, cast on 96 stitches. Place single color marker and join in the round, being careful not to twist stitches.

Work (k1, p1) rib pattern for approximately 1½ to 2 in. / 4 to 5 cm.

Switch to larger needles and work chart from right to left beginning on Row 1, bottom right corner. Chart repeats three times around the hat. Use remaining two stitch markers of another color to mark chart repeats.

Note: In order to avoid long "floats" (strands of yarn on the inside of the hat) and to help maintain your tension, do not carry a color more than three or four stitches without twisting the colors around each other in the back of work.

Switch to DPNs when work becomes too small for circular needles.

FINISHING

After chart is complete, cut yarn, leaving a 10 in. / 25.5 cm tail. Using a tapestry needle, weave tail through remaining stitches and pull tightly to close circle. Pull tail to inside and weave in all ends.

Block as desired. See page 13 for my favorite hat blocking technique.

Duplicate stitching: If desired, add duplicate stitched "painted trim" around the doors and windows using a tapestry needle and color C or any other trim color of your choice. Add French knot flowers around the base of the building. Attach lantern-shaped charms to building using needle and thread. Placement is optional. See photos for inspiration. "Two if by sea" adds a bit of history, even if it's not the Old North Church.

KEY

☐ K
Knit

D Dup
Work duplicate stitches after all knitting and blocking is complete.

⧅ ssk
Slip 2 stitches knitwise, then knit slipped stitches together through back loop

■ No Stitch
The "no stitch" squares represent the stitches that were lost due to decreases earlier in the round. *Do not skip a stitch.* Simply treat these squares as if they do not exist.

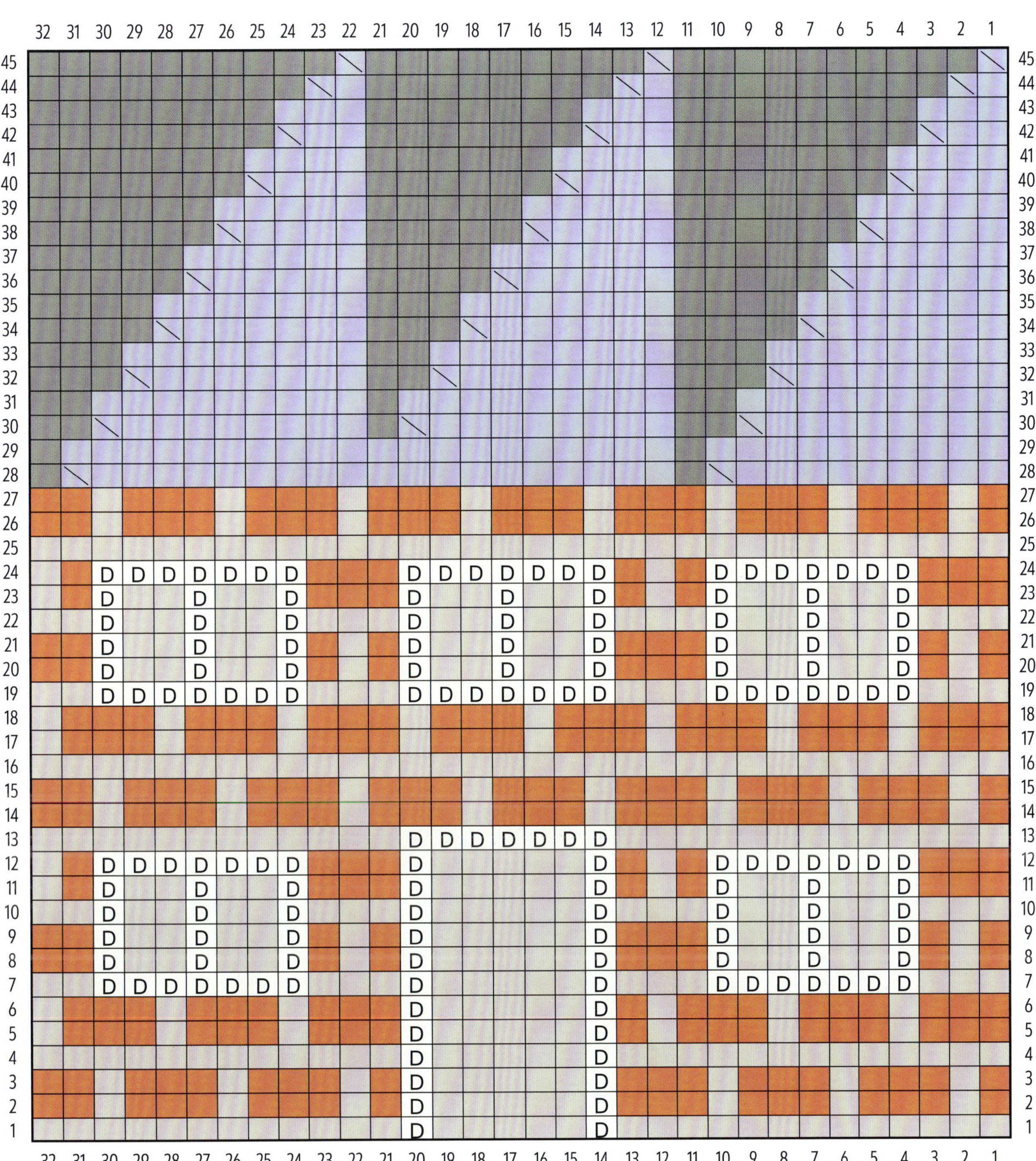

Much of New Hampshire—nicknamed the Granite State—is covered in beautiful and heavily forested mountains and hills with an abundance of wildlife. Granite peaks, rock formations, gorges, and cliffs that dot the state (along with rivers and lakes) have created spectacular places to explore and enjoy the scenery. In the famous Flume Gorge, visitors can walk along a wooden boardwalk next to a river between vertical granite cliffs. Just beautiful! Each season in New Hampshire brings something new to celebrate with festivals and community events: snow sculpting in winter, maple sugaring in spring, lupines and butterflies in summer, and the changing of the leaves in the fall. New Hampshire's fall foliage is legendary as the hillsides turn bright orange and leaf peepers from around the country visit their favorite locations, including the famed Kancamagus Scenic Byway.

The beauty of a red fox against the white and gray of a harsh winter is captured in this design. A band of tracks in the snow adds a bit of whimsy.

SIZE

One size fits an average adult size head (approx. 19 in. / 48 cm – 22 in. / 56 cm)

Finished Circumference: approx. 20¼ in. / 51.5 cm.

YARN

Worsted weight yarn (#4) in four colors. Shown in:

- **A:** Malabrigo Rios: Natural (50 g / 105 yd. / 96 m)
- **B:** Stunning String Studio Legacy Worsted: Shadow (13 g / 28 yd. / 26 m)
- **C:** Peekaboo Yarns Merino Worsted: Silverstone (33 g/ 72 yd. / 66 m)
- **D:** Aly Bee Workshop Merino Worsted: Carrot Cake (20 g / 40 yd. / 37 m)

NEEDLES

- US size 5 / 3.75 mm, 16 in. / 40 cm circular knitting needles
- US size 7 / 4.5 mm, 16 in. / 40 cm circular knitting needles
- US size 7 / 4.5 mm, set of double-pointed needles (DPNs)
- (or size needed to obtain gauge)

Continued on next page

NOTIONS

3 stitch markers (two of one color and one of another color)

Tapestry needle for weaving in ends and working duplicate stitches

Yarn or faux-fur pom-pom (optional)

GAUGE

With larger needles, approx. 9½ stitches = 2 in. / 5 cm in stranded stockinette stitch, blocked.

Note: If you already know you are a tight knitter (or just want a larger hat), go up one or two needle sizes for both the ribbing and the body of the hat.

With smaller circular needles and color A, cast on 96 stitches. Place single color marker and join in the round, being careful not to twist stitches.

Work (k1, p1) rib pattern for approximately 4 in. / 10 cm for a fold-over ribbing/brim as shown.

Switch to larger needles and work chart from right to left beginning on Row 1, bottom right corner. Chart repeats three times around the hat. Use remaining two stitch markers of another color to mark chart repeats.

Note: In order to avoid long “floats” (strands of yarn on the inside of the hat) and to help maintain your tension, do not carry a color more than three to four stitches without twisting the colors around each other in the back of work.

Switch to DPNs when work becomes too small for circular needles.

FINISHING

After chart is complete, cut yarn leaving, a 10 in. / 25.5 cm tail. Using a tapestry needle, weave tail through remaining stitches and pull tightly to close circle. Pull tail to inside and weave in all ends.

Block as desired. See page 13 for my favorite hat blocking technique.

After all knitting and blocking is complete, work duplicate stitches where shown using a tapestry needle. Add eyes to the foxes using French knots in color B.

Optional: Attach a yarn or faux-fur pom-pom to top of hat. I chose a pom-pom that resembles fox fur.

KEY

☐ K
Knit

D Dup
Work duplicate stitches after all knitting and blocking is complete.

/ K2tog
Knit 2 together

■ No Stitch
The “no stitch” squares represent the stitches that were lost due to decreases earlier in the round. *Do not skip a stitch.* Simply treat these squares as if they do not exist.

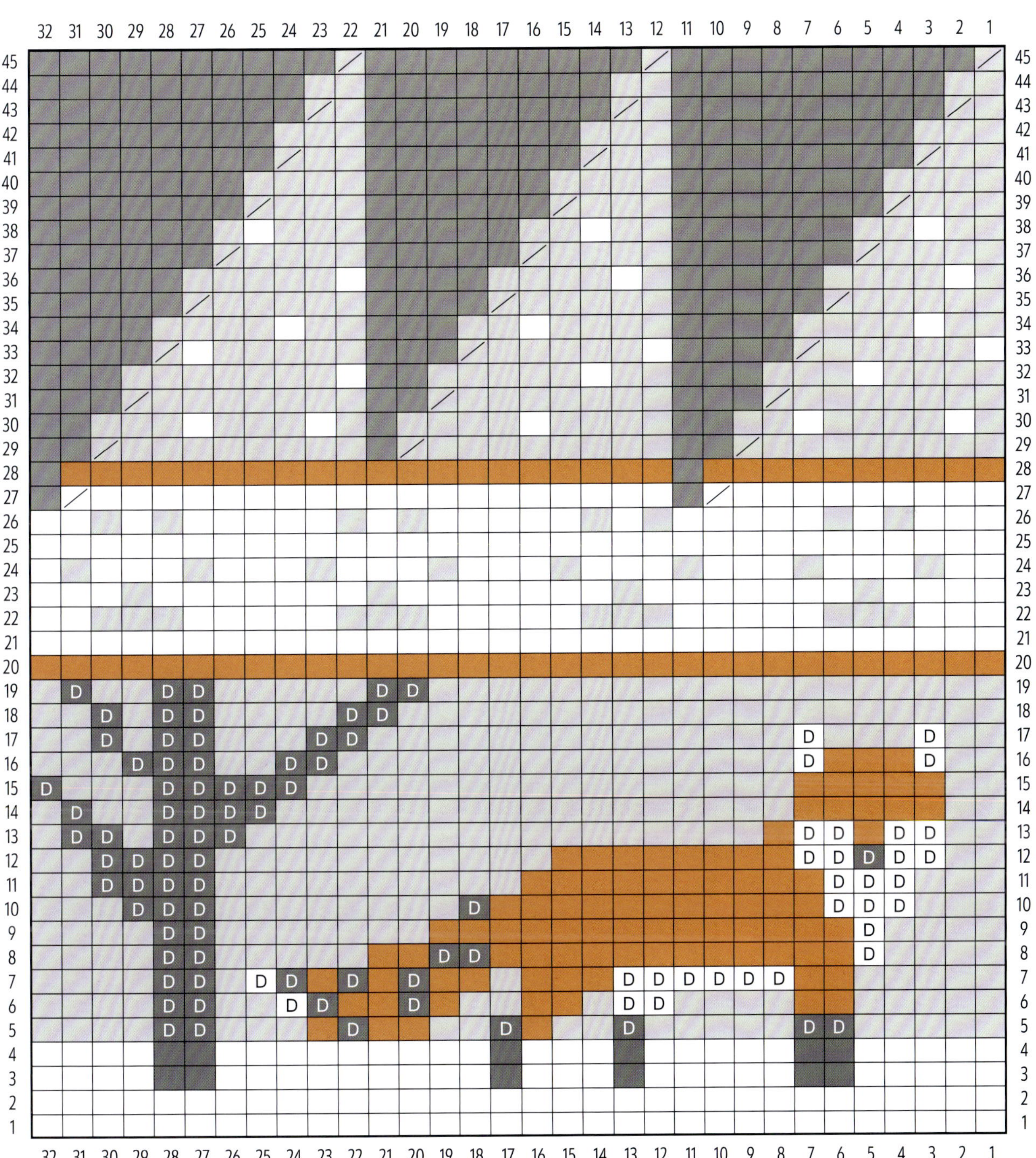
32 31 30 29 28 27 26 25 24 23 22 21 20 19 18 17 16 15 14 13 12 11 10 9 8 7 6 5 4 3 2 1
45 44 43 42 41 40 39 38 37 36 35 34 33 32 31 30 29 28 27 26 25 24 23 22 21 20 19 18 17 16 15 14 13 12 11 10 9 8 7 6 5 4 3 2 1

Despite being the most densely populated and one of the most urbanized of all fifty states, much of New Jersey is covered in forests. This comes as a surprise to most outsiders. With miles and miles of beaches and boardwalks, the shore regions of New Jersey reign supreme in popularity and tourism. Restaurants, water parks, thrill rides, shopping, water activities, historic sites, and so much more provide endless entertainment, recreation, and relaxation for locals and tourists alike.

But this design focuses on another group of locals—the wildlife of the forests and lakes! Black bears, racoons, and trout make a slightly understated appearance in this playful design, featuring wildlife-inspired colors. It's as though the animals are peering from their world into yours. Using buttons for eyes adds a bit of life to the design.

SIZE

One size fits an average adult size head (approx. 19 in. / 48 cm – 22 in. / 56 cm)

Finished Circumference: approx. 20¼ in. / 51.5 cm.

YARN

Worsted weight yarn (#4) in seven colors. Shown in:

- **A:** Malabrigo Rios: Black (15 g / 32 yd. / 29 m)
- **B:** Peekaboo Yarns Merino Worsted: Zion Blue (15 g / 32 yd. / 29 m)
- **C:** Stunning String Studio Legacy Worsted: Shadow (20 g / 43 yd./ 39 m)
- **D:** *Stunning String Studio Legacy Worsted: Dried Hops (approx. 3 yd. / 2.75 m)
- **E:** Apple Fiber Studio Apple Crisp: Latte Foam (15 g / 32 yd. / 29 m)
- **F:** Polka Dot Sheep Whitefish Worsted: Scenic Byway (50 g / 109 yd./ 100 m)
- **G:** Polka Dot Sheep Whitefish Worsted: Stageline (15 g / 32 yd. / 29 m)

*Used only in duplicate stitching

Continued on next page

NEEDLES

- US size 5 / 3.75 mm, 16 in. / 40 cm circular knitting needles
- US size 7 / 4.5 mm, 16 in. / 40 cm circular knitting needles
- US size 7 / 4.5 mm, set of double-pointed needles (DPNs)
- (or size needed to obtain gauge)

NOTIONS

12–15 beads for eyes of wildlife.

3 stitch markers (two of one color and one of another color)

Tapestry needle for weaving in ends and working duplicate stitches

Faux fur pom-pom (optional)

GAUGE

With larger needles, approx. 9½ stitches = 2 in. / 5 cm in stranded stockinette stitch, blocked.

Note: If you already know you are a tight knitter (or just want a larger hat), go up one or two needle sizes for both the ribbing and the body of the hat.

With smaller circular needles and color F, cast on 96 stitches. Place single color marker and join in the round, being careful not to twist stitches.

Work (k2, p2) rib pattern for approximately 4 in. / 10 cm for a fold-over ribbing/brim as shown, or 1½ to 2 in. / 4 to 5 cm for a single ribbing/brim.

Switch to larger needles and work chart from right to left beginning on Row 1, bottom right corner. Chart repeats three times around the hat. Use remaining two stitch markers of another color to mark chart repeats.

Note: In order to avoid long “floats” (strands of yarn on the inside of the hat) and to help maintain your tension, do not carry a color more than three or four stitches without twisting the colors around each other in the back of work.

Switch to DPNs when work becomes too small for circular needles.

FINISHING

After chart is complete, cut yarn leaving a 10 in. / 25.5 cm tail. Using a tapestry needle, weave tail through remaining stitches and pull tightly to close circle. Pull tail to inside and weave in all ends.

Block as desired. See page 13 for my favorite hat blocking technique.

After all blocking is complete, work duplicate stitches in the colors and locations shown.

Optional: Sew on beads for the eyes of the bears and raccoons using 1 to 4 plies of black yarn. See photos for inspiration. Leave the trout eyes as is or add beads. Optional: Add faux fur pom-pom.

KEY

☐ K
Knit

[D] Dup
Work duplicate stitches after all knitting and blocking is complete.

[•] P
Purl

[/] K2tog
Knit 2 together

■ No Stitch
The “no stitch” squares represent the stitches that were lost due to decreases earlier in the round. *Do not skip a stitch*. Simply treat these squares as if they do not exist.

New York City is one of the most famous and recognizable cities in the world. One glimpse of the Empire State Building, Statue of Liberty, or Times Square and there's no mistaking where you are. But head upstate and the entire vibe changes from bustling city to relaxing countryside. Small towns, hamlets, forests, rivers, and lakes welcome you to what the rest of this beautiful state has to offer. The green forests of the Hudson River Valley, Catskills, Finger Lakes, and Adirondacks are perfect for spring and summer adventures. But as autumn temperatures cool, the colors of the landscape heat up with the oranges, yellows, and reds of fall foliage, making for some spectacular siteseeing. Toss in a visit to a corn maze or some delicious cider donuts, and the cozy adventures of autumn in New York are complete.

This design features the warmth of fall colors from the city skyline up to the textured trees, the blue of lakes and rivers, and the evergreen forests.

SIZE

One size fits an average adult size head (approx. 19 in. / 48 cm – 22 in. / 56 cm)

Finished Circumference: approx. 20¼ in. / 51.5 cm.

YARN

Worsted weight yarn (#4) in five colors. Shown in:

- **A:** Aly Bee Workshop Merino Worsted: Maple Leaf (33 g / 66 yd./ 60 m)
- **B:** Malabrigo Rios: Plomo (15 g / 32 yd. / 29 m)
- **C:** Dragonfly Fibers and Canon Hand Dyes Sylph Worsted: Cloudy Sky (20 g / 35 yd./ 32 m)
- **D:** Polka Dot Sheep Whitefish Worsted: Moose Meadow (10 g / 21 yd./ 19 m)
- **E:** Malabrigo Rios: Denim (10 g/ 21 yd./ 19 m)

Continued on next page

NEEDLES

- US size 5 / 3.75 mm, 16 in. / 40 cm circular knitting needles
- US size 7 / 4.5 mm, 16 in. / 40 cm circular knitting needles
- US size 7 / 4.5 mm, set of double-pointed needles (DPNs)
- (or size needed to obtain gauge)

NOTIONS

3 stitch markers (two of one color and one of another color)

Tapestry needle for weaving in ends

GAUGE

With larger needles, approx. 9½ stitches = 2 in. / 5 cm in stranded stockinette stitch, blocked.

Note: If you already know you are a tight knitter (or just want a larger hat), go up one or two needle sizes for both the ribbing and the body of the hat.

With smaller circular needles and color A, cast on 96 stitches. Place single color marker and join in the round, being careful not to twist stitches.

Work (k1, p1) rib pattern for approximately 1½ to 2 in. / 4 to 5 cm.

Switch to larger needles and work chart from right to left beginning on Row 1, bottom right corner. Chart repeats three times around the hat. Use remaining two stitch markers of another color to mark chart repeats.

Note: In order to avoid long "floats" (strands of yarn on the inside of the hat) and to help maintain your tension, do not carry a color more than three or four stitches without twisting the colors around each other in the back of work.

Switch to DPNs when work becomes too small for circular needles.

FINISHING

After chart is complete, cut yarn leaving a 10 in. / 25.5 cm tail. Using a tapestry needle, weave tail through remaining stitches and pull tightly to close circle. Pull tail to inside and weave in all ends.

Block as desired. See page 13 for my favorite hat blocking technique.

KEY

☐ K
Knit

⊡ P
Purl

⧄ K2tog
Knit 2 together

■ No Stitch
The "no stitch" squares represent the stitches that were lost due to decreases earlier in the round. *Do not skip a stitch.* Simply treat these squares as if they do not exist.

⧄ P2tog
Purl 2 together

Did you know that Pennsylvania has more covered bridges than any other state? The nostalgic charm of these bridges evokes a bygone era, making them a sought-after subject for photographers and travelers with a love of history. It's estimated that more than ten thousand covered bridges were built across the United States by the late 1870s with roughly six hundred still standing today. Around two hundred of these are in Pennsylvania. Covering a wooden bridge not only made it look more attractive, it also offered protection from rain and snow, prolonging the life of the bridge by decades. As a bonus, these sturdy structures also served as shelters for weary travelers or livestock—or as a location to meet up with a friend.

This design captures the nostalgic scene of covered bridges across a meandering river on a sunny autumn day.

SIZE

One size fits an average adult size head (approx. 19 in. / 48 cm – 22 in. / 56 cm)

Finished Circumference: approx. 20¼ in. / 51.5 cm.

YARN

Worsted weight yarn (#4) in ten colors. Shown in:

Colors used in knitting:

- **A:** Ewe 2 Yarn Mellow Worsted: Fallen (25 g / 54 yd. / 49 m)
- **B:** Stunning String Studio Legacy Worsted: Big Sky (15 g / 32 yd. / 29m)
- **C:** Comfort and Joy Yarn Co. Cheer: Paprika (10 g / 21 yd. / 19 m)
- **D:** Peekaboo Yarns Merino Worsted: Cuyahoga Foliage (15 g / 32 yd. / 29 m)
- **E:** Malabrigo Rios: Tormenta (10 g / 21 yd. / 19 m)
- **F:** Aly Bee Workshop Merino Worsted: Maple Leaf (20 g / 43 yd. / 39 m)
- **G:** Aly Bee Workshop Merino Worsted: Marble Soda (20 g / 43 yd. / 39 m)

Colors used only in duplicate stitching:

- **H:** Malabrigo Rios: Cape Cod Gray (10 g / 21 yd ./ 19 m)
- **I:** Malabrigo Rios: Natural (5 g / 11 yd. / 10 m)
- **J:** Stunning String Studio Legacy Worsted: Shadow (5 g / 11 yd. / 10 m)

Continued on next page

NEEDLES

- US size 5 / 3.75 mm, 16 in. / 40 cm circular knitting needles
- US size 7 / 4.5 mm, 16 in. / 40 cm circular knitting needles
- US size 7 / 4.5 mm, set of double-pointed needles (DPNs)
- (or size needed to obtain gauge)

NOTIONS

3 stitch markers (two of one color and one of another color)

Tapestry needle for weaving in ends and working duplicate stitches and embroidery

GAUGE

With larger needles, approx. 9½ stitches = 2 in. / 5 cm in stranded stockinette stitch, blocked.

Note: If you already know you are a tight knitter (or just want a larger hat), go up one or two needle sizes for both the ribbing and the body of the hat.

With smaller circular needles and color A, cast on 96 stitches. Place single color marker and join in the round, being careful not to twist stitches.

Work (k1, p1) rib pattern for approximately 1½ to 2 in. / 4 to 5 cm.

Switch to larger needles and work chart from right to left beginning on Row 1, bottom right corner. Chart repeats three times around the hat. Use remaining two stitch markers of another color to mark chart repeats.

Note: In order to avoid long "floats" (strands of yarn on the inside of the hat) and to help maintain your tension, do not carry a color more than three or four stitches without twisting the colors around each other in the back of work.

Switch to DPNs when work becomes too small for circular needles.

FINISHING

After chart is complete, cut yarn leaving a 10 in. / 25.5 cm tail. Using a tapestry needle, weave tail through remaining stitches and pull tightly to close circle. Pull tail to inside and weave in all ends.

Block as desired. See page 13 for my favorite hat blocking technique.

Duplicate stitching: After all blocking is complete, work all duplicate stitches in the colors and locations shown on chart.

Optional: Using only 2 plies of the 4-ply yarn in Natural, add "trim" around the windows using simple straight stitches. See photo for inspiration.

KEY

☐ K
Knit

[D] Dup
Work duplicate stitches after all knitting and blocking is complete.

[/] K2tog
Knit 2 together

■ No Stitch
The "no stitch" squares represent the stitches that were lost due to decreases earlier in the round. *Do not skip a stitch.* Simply treat these squares as if they do not exist.

Nicknamed the Ocean State, Rhode Island is only forty-eight miles long and thirty-seven miles wide, but it still boasts nearly four hundred miles of coastline. How is this possible? Narragansett Bay, dotted with many small islands, runs through much of the state, significantly increasing the coastline. This means that almost every Rhode Islander lives within a thirty-minute drive to the coast. With such a connection to the sea, Rhode Island features an abundance of quaint coastal towns, historic sites, delectable seafood, beautiful beaches, and a rich maritime history with a strong tradition of sailing. The protection of the bay and just-right breezes have made this tiny state an ideal location for sailing schools, yacht clubs, and sea-inspired tourism, as well as a starting point for many well-known sailing events.

Marinas filled with sailing vessels of all sizes—the inspiration for this fun design—are a common sight in Rhode Island. A touch of simple embroidery adds details to the boats and seagulls in the sky.

SIZE

One size fits an average adult size head (approx. 19 in. / 48 cm – 22 in. / 56 cm)

Finished Circumference: approx. 20¼ in. / 51.5 cm.

YARN

Worsted weight yarn (#4) in five colors. Shown in:

- **A:** Storyteller Stitchery Fable: Winter in Concord (33 g / 72 yd./ 66 m)
- **B:** Aly Bee Workshop Merino Worsted: Vanilla (20 g / 43 yd. / 39 m)
- **C:** Stunning String Studio Legacy Worsted: Gothic Brick (10 g / 21 yd. / 19 m)
- **D:** Stunning String Studio Legacy Worsted: Black Forest (10 g / 21 yd. / 19 m)
- **E:** Stunning String Studio Legacy Worsted: Cloudy Sky (20 g/ 43 yd./ 39 m)

NEEDLES

- US size 5 / 3.75 mm, 16 in. / 40 cm circular knitting needles
- US size 7 / 4.5 mm, 16 in. / 40 cm circular knitting needles
- US size 7 / 4.5 mm, set of double-pointed needles (DPNs)
- (or size needed to obtain gauge)

Continued on next page

NOTIONS

3 stitch markers (two of one color and one of another color)

Tapestry needle for weaving in ends and working duplicate stitches and embroidery

GAUGE

With larger needles, approx. 9½ stitches = 2 in. / 5 cm in stranded stockinette stitch, blocked.

Note: If you already know you are a tight knitter (or just want a larger hat), go up one or two needle sizes for both the ribbing and the body of the hat.

With smaller circular needles and color A, cast on 96 stitches. Place single color marker and join in the round, being careful not to twist stitches.

Work (k1 tbl, p1) rib pattern for approximately 1½ to 2 in. / 4 to 5 cm.
(tbl=through back loop)

Switch to larger needles and work chart from right to left beginning on Row 1, bottom right corner. Chart repeats three times around the hat. Use remaining two stitch markers of another color to mark chart repeats.

Note: In order to avoid long "floats" (strands of yarn on the inside of the hat) and to help maintain your tension, do not carry a color more than three or four stitches without twisting the colors around each other in the back of work.

Switch to DPNs when work becomes too small for circular needles.

FINISHING

After chart is complete, cut yarn leaving a 10 in. / 25.5 cm tail. Using a tapestry needle, weave tail through remaining stitches and pull tightly to close circle. Pull tail to inside and weave in all ends.

Block as desired. See page 13 for my favorite hat blocking technique.

After all knitting and blocking is complete, work duplicate stitches where shown using a tapestry needle. Add "masts" to as many boats as desired using long straight stitches tacked down with tiny straight stitches. Add seagulls as desired using same method. For the birds, the small stitch used to tack down the longer stitch becomes the body. See photos for inspiration.

KEY

☐ **K** — Knit

D **Dup** — Work duplicate stitches after all knitting and blocking is complete.

V **S1** — Slip one purlwise with yarn in back

/ **K2tog** — Knit 2 together

■ **No Stitch** — The "no stitch" squares represent the stitches that were lost due to decreases earlier in the round. *Do not skip a stitch.* Simply treat these squares as if they do not exist.

There's nothing quite so magical as standing on a hillside, gazing out at an orange-and-yellow landscape while autumn leaves swirl in the breeze around you. Welcome to autumn in Vermont! This New England state is beautiful and fun-filled in any season: world-class snow activities in winter, then hiking the Green Mountains, biking the famous Stowe Recreation Path, and exploring lovely small towns, apple orchards, and covered bridges in any of the other three seasons. Each season has something special to offer, but it's the oranges, yellows, and reds of autumn that cover the hillsides, surround waterfalls, line lakes and rivers, and turn every scene into painting-worthy views that stand out as classic Vermont. The cider donuts, corn mazes, and cozy inns are a welcome bonus to this already amazing fall destination.

The countryside of Vermont is represented by the beautiful colors of fall worked in a variety of easy-to-knit Fair Isle patterns, including leaf-inspired motifs.

SIZE

One size fits an average adult size head (approx. 19 in. / 48 cm – 22 in. / 56 cm)

Finished Circumference: approx. 20¼ in. / 51.5 cm.

YARN

Worsted weight yarn (#4) in five colors. Shown in:

Aly Bee Workshop Merino Worsted:

- **A:** Dill Pickle (10 g / 20 yd. / 18 m)
- **B:** Honey Bee (20 g / 40 yd. / 37 m)
- **C:** Pumpkin Spice (20 g / 40 yd. / 37 m)
- **D:** Farmhouse (15 g / 30 yd. / 27 m))
- **E:** Maple Leaf (25 g / 50 yd. / 46 m)

Continued on next page

NEEDLES

- US size 5 / 3.75 mm, 16 in. / 40 cm circular knitting needles
- US size 7 / 4.5 mm, 16 in. / 40 cm circular knitting needles
- US size 7 / 4.5 mm, set of double-pointed needles (DPNs)
- (or size needed to obtain gauge)

NOTIONS

3 stitch markers (two of one color and one of another color)

Tapestry needle for weaving in ends

GAUGE

With larger needles, approx. 9½ stitches = 2 in. / 5 cm in stranded stockinette stitch, blocked.

Note: If you already know you are a tight knitter (or just want a larger hat), go up one or two needle sizes for both the ribbing and the body of the hat.

With smaller circular needles and color E, cast on 96 stitches. Place single color marker and join in the round, being careful not to twist stitches.

Work (k1, p1) rib pattern for approximately 1½ to 2 in. / 4 to 5 cm.

Switch to larger needles and work chart from right to left beginning on Row 1, bottom right corner. Chart repeats three times around the hat. Use remaining two stitch markers of another color to mark chart repeats.

Switch to DPNs when work becomes too small for circular needles.

FINISHING

After chart is complete, cut yarn leaving a 10 in. / 25.5 cm tail. Using a tapestry needle, weave tail through remaining stitches and pull tightly to close circle. Pull tail to inside and weave in all ends.

Block as desired. See page 13 for my favorite hat blocking technique.

KEY

□ **K** Knit

⧄ **K2tog** Knit 2 together

■ **No Stitch** The "no stitch" squares represent the stitches that were lost due to decreases earlier in the round. *Do not skip a stitch.* Simply treat these squares as if they do not exist.

THE SOUTH

Alabama

Arkansas

Florida

Georgia

Kentucky

Louisiana

Mississippi

North Carolina

South Carolina

Tennessee

Virginia

West Virginia

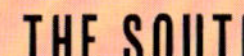

Alabama's unique biodiversity supports a multitude of interesting plant and animal life as well as a thriving agricultural industry, beautiful scenery, and a wide range of recreational opportunities. Alligators, black bears, snakes, and bobcats are equally at home in Alabama. What a variety! From caves and waterfalls to mountains and prairies, there's something for everyone in this Southern state.

Using subtle texture and nature-inspired colors, this design takes you from white sand beaches on the Gulf Coast to the shore of a rippling river, the diagonal rows of crops, and up to the forests of the southern Appalachians. Fun fact: Alabama has more turtle species than any other state! This is the perfect hat to spread a little turtle love with a turtle shaped button.

SIZE

One size fits an average adult size head (approx. 19 in. / 48 cm – 22 in. / 56 cm)

Finished Circumference: approx. 20¼ in. / 51.5 cm.

YARN

- **A:** Ewe 2 Yarn Mellow Worsted: Breeze (25 g / 54 yd. / 49 m)
- **B:** Malabrigo Rios: Natural (10 g / 21 yd. / 19 m)
- **C:** Stunning String Studio Legacy Worsted: Black Forest (15 g / 32 yd. / 29 m)
- **D:** Malabrigo Rios: Lettuce (15 g / 32 yd. / 29 m)
- **E:** Storyteller Stitchery Fable: Winter in Concord (15 g / 32 yd. / 29 m)
- **F:** Malabrigo Rios: Aquamarine (15 g / 32 yd. / 29 m)

Continued on next page

NEEDLES

- US size 5 / 3.75 mm, 16 in. / eedles
- US size 7 / 4.5 mm, 16 in. / 40 cm circular knitting needles
- US size 7 / 4.5 mm, set of double-pointed needles (DPNs)

(or size needed to obtain gauge)

NOTIONS

3 stitch markers (two of one color and one of another color)

Tapestry needle for weaving in ends

GAUGE

With larger needles, approx. 9½ stitches = 2 in. / 5 cm in stranded stockinette stitch, blocked.

Note: If you already know you are a tight knitter (or just want a larger hat), go up one or two needle sizes for both the ribbing and the body of the hat.

With smaller circular needles and color A, cast on 96 stitches. Place single color marker and join in the round, being careful not to twist stitches.

Work (k1, p1) rib pattern for approximately 1½ to 2 in. / 4 to 5 cm.

Switch to larger needles and work chart from right to left beginning on Row 1, bottom right corner. Chart repeats three times around the hat. Use remaining two stitch markers of another color to mark chart repeats.

Switch to DPNs when work becomes too small for circular needles.

FINISHING

After chart is complete, cut yarn leaving a 10 in. / 25.5 cm tail. Using a tapestry needle, weave tail through remaining stitches and pull tightly to close circle. Pull tail to inside and weave in all ends.

Block as desired. See page 13 for my favorite hat blocking technique.

KEY

☐ K
Knit

⊡ P
Purl

⧄ K2tog
Knit 2 together

■ No Stitch
The "no stitch" squares represent the stitches that were lost due to decreases earlier in the round. *Do not skip a stitch.* Simply treat these squares as if they do not exist.

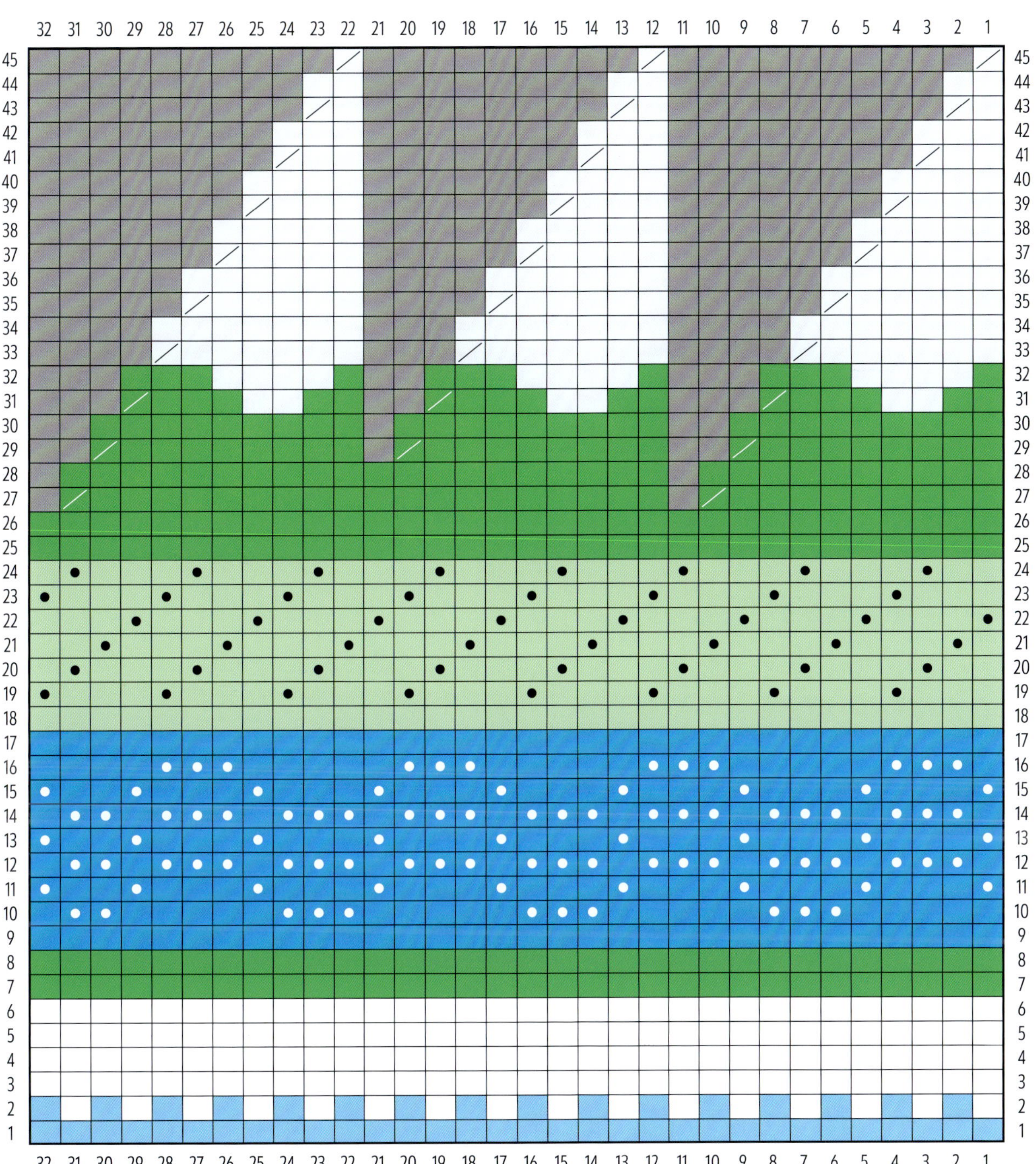

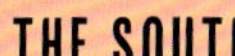

Trees—as far as the eye can see! From the Ozark Mountains to the West Gulf Coastal Plain, almost 60 percent of Arkansas is considered forestland. With more than 180 different types of trees (a mix of evergreen and deciduous), the color of the landscape changes seasonally from bright or deep greens to a kaleidoscope of vibrant oranges, yellows, and reds. Viewing the beautiful landscape from one of many lookout towers is a popular tourist attraction, especially from the 216-foot-tall Hot Springs Mountain Tower in Hot Springs National Park.

This design features subtle, easy-to-knit texture in three shades of green reminiscent of a tree-covered landscape in spring or summer. As an alternative, use shades of oranges, reds, or yellows for a fall landscape.

SIZE

One size fits an average adult size head (approx. 19 in. / 48 cm – 22 in. / 56 cm)

Finished Circumference: approx. 20¼ in. / 51.5 cm.

YARN

Worsted weight yarn (#4) in three colors. Shown in:

- **A:** Malabrigo Rios: Lettuce (50 g / 105 yd. / 96 m)
- **B:** Stunning String Studio Legacy Worsted: Rosemary (25 g / 54 yd. / 49 m)
- **C:** Dragonfly Fibers and Canon Hand Dyes Sylph Worsted: Into the Woods (25 g / 44 yd. / 40 m)

These amounts DO include enough yarn for a tri-color pom-pom.

Continued on next page

NEEDLES

- US size 5 / 3.75 mm, 16 in. / 40 cm circular knitting needles
- US size 7 / 4.5 mm, 16 in. / 40 cm circular knitting needles
- US size 7 / 4.5 mm, set of double-pointed needles (DPNs)
- (or size needed to obtain gauge)

NOTIONS

3 stitch markers (two of one color and one of another color)

Tapestry needle for weaving in ends.

GAUGE

With larger needles, approx. 9½ stitches = 2 in. / 5 cm in stranded stockinette stitch, blocked.

Note: If you already know you are a tight knitter (or just want a larger hat), go up one or two needle sizes for both the ribbing and the body of the hat.

With smaller circular needles and color A, cast on 96 stitches. Place single color marker and join in the round, being careful not to twist stitches.

Work (k1, p1) rib pattern for approximately 1½ to 2 in. / 4 to 5 cm.

Increase Round: *K31, kfb; repeat from * 2 more times - 99 sts total.

Switch to larger needles and work chart from right to left beginning on Row 1, bottom right corner. Chart repeats three times around the hat. Use remaining two stitch markers of another color to mark chart repeats.

Note: In order to avoid long "floats" (strands of yarn on the inside of the hat) and to help maintain your tension, do not carry a color more than three or four stitches without twisting the colors around each other in the back of work.

Switch to DPNs when work becomes too small for circular needles.

FINISHING

After chart is complete, cut yarn leaving a 10 in. / 25.5 cm tail. Using a tapestry needle, weave tail through remaining stitches and pull tightly to close circle. Pull tail to inside and weave in all ends.

Block as desired. See page 13 for my favorite hat blocking technique.

Optional: Using your favorite method, make a pom-pom using all three colors. Attach to top of beanie.

KEY

☐	K Knit
•	P Purl
/	K2tog Knit 2 together
■	No Stitch The "no stitch" squares represent the stitches that were lost due to decreases earlier in the round. *Do not skip a stitch*. Simply treat these squares as if they do not exist.
·/	P2tog Purl 2 together

When people think of Florida, they often think of theme parks, the space industry, cultural diversity, or something that has to do with water. Considering most of the state is bordered by the Atlantic Ocean and the Gulf of Mexico, this makes sense. Beaches lined with palm trees, an abundance of marinas, and freshwater springs, lakes, and rivers mean that almost every Floridian lives or vacations near water. For tourists and locals alike, there's nothing quite iconically Florida as kayaking near coastal mangrove forests or the thrill of an airboat ride through wetlands with egrets and herons overhead. From alligators, sea turtles, and manatees to panthers and flamingos, even the wildlife in Florida seems tropical and exotic compared to other states.

The beloved Florida manatees are the stars of this design. These protected marine mammals are large, slow moving, gentle, whisker-bearing herbivores. What's not to love?

SIZE

One size fits an average adult size head (approx. 19 in. / 48 cm – 22 in. / 56 cm)

Finished Circumference: approx. 20¼ in. / 51.5 cm.

YARN

Worsted weight yarn (#4) in four colors. Shown in:

- **A:** Berroco Vintage: 5162 Envy (25 g / 55 yd. / 50 m)
- **B:** Berroco Vintage: 5116 Dove (20 g / 44 yd. / 40 m)
- **C:** Berroco Vintage: 51134 Horizon Blue (25 g / 55 yd. / 50 m)
- **D:** Berroco Vintage: 5197 Neptune (20 g / 44 yd. / 40 m)

NEEDLES

- US size 5 / 3.75 mm, 16 in. / 40 cm circular knitting needles
- US size 7 / 4.5 mm, 16 in. / 40 cm circular knitting needles
- US size 7 / 4.5 mm, set of double-pointed needles (DPNs)
- (or size needed to obtain gauge)

Continued on next page

NOTIONS

Optional: Beads for the eyes of the manatees.

3 stitch markers (two of one color and one of another color)

Tapestry needle for weaving in ends and working duplicate stitches and embroidery

GAUGE

With larger needles, approx. 9½ stitches = 2 in. / 5 cm in stranded stockinette stitch, blocked.

Note: If you already know you are a tight knitter (or just want a larger hat), go up one or two needle sizes for both the ribbing and the body of the hat.

With smaller circular needles and color A, cast on 96 stitches. Place single color marker and join in the round, being careful not to twist stitches.

Work (k1, p1) rib pattern for approximately 1½ to 2 in. / 4 to 5 cm.

Switch to larger needles and work chart from right to left beginning on Row 1, bottom right corner. Chart repeats three times around the hat. Use remaining two stitch markers of another color to mark chart repeats.

Note: In order to avoid long "floats" (strands of yarn on the inside of the hat) and to help maintain your tension, do not carry a color more than three or four stitches without twisting the colors around each other in the back of work.

Switch to DPNs when work becomes too small for circular needles.

FINISHING

After chart is complete, cut yarn leaving a 10 in. / 25.5 cm tail. Using a tapestry needle, weave tail through remaining stitches and pull tightly to close circle. Pull tail to inside and weave in all ends.

Block as desired. See page 13 for my favorite hat blocking technique.

After all knitting and blocking is complete, work duplicate stitches in the colors and locations shown on chart.

Optional: Use French knots or sewn-on small beads to add eyes to the manatees.

KEY

☐ K
Knit

D Dup
Work duplicate stitches after all knitting and blocking is complete.

⧄ K2tog
Knit 2 together

■ No Stitch
The "no stitch" squares represent the stitches that were lost due to decreases earlier in the round. *Do not skip a stitch*. Simply treat these squares as if they do not exist.

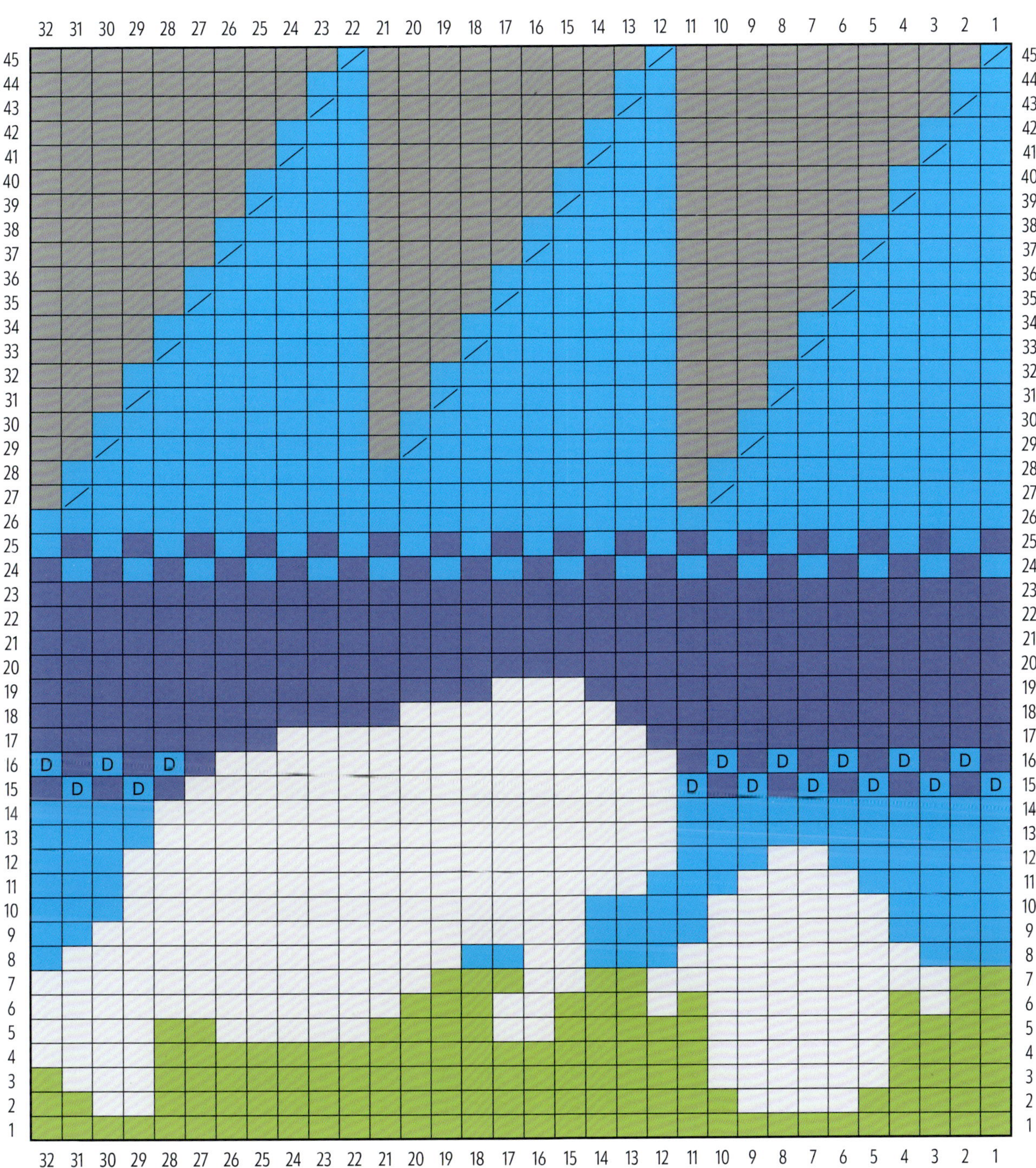
D

Whether they're baked into pies and cobblers, cooked into jam, mixed into ice cream, or eaten fresh off a tree, no other fruit captures the essence of summer quite like a fresh, juicy peach. Arguably some of the freshest and juciest peaches of all come from Georgia, known as the Peach State. A summer vacation in Georgia might start with historical sites, museums, scenic drives, nature trails, tasty Southern dishes, or a trip to the beach, but it just might end with a peachy treat from a farmers market, roadside stand, or even a peach festival.

Fresh, summery colors feature bands of pink peach blossoms and fully ripened peaches in this design.

SIZE

One size fits an average adult size head (approx. 19 in. / 48 cm – 22 in. / 56 cm)

Finished Circumference: approx. 20¼ in. / 51.5 cm.

YARN

Worsted weight yarn (#4) in six colors. Shown in:

- **A:** Malabrigo Rios: Natural (25 g / 53 yd. / 48 m)
- **B:** Aly Bee Workshop Merino Worsted: Nectarine (25 g / 50 yd. / 46 m)
- **C:** Aly Bee Workshop Merino Worsted: Maple Leaf (10 g / 20 yd. / 18 m)
- **D:** Stunning String Studio Legacy Worsted: Pine Bough (25 g / 54 yd. / 49 m)
- **E:** Stunning String Studio Legacy Worsted: Zinfandel (5 g / 11 yd. / 10 m)
- **F:** *Stunning String Studio Legacy Worsted: Cranberries (approx. 3–4 yd. / 2.75-3 m)

* Used only in duplicate stitching

Continued on next page

NEEDLES

- US size 5 / 3.75 mm, 16 in. / 40 cm circular knitting needles
- US size 7 / 4.5 mm, 16 in. / 40 cm circular knitting needles
- US size 7 / 4.5 mm, set of double-pointed needles (DPNs)
- (or size needed to obtain gauge)

NOTIONS

3 stitch markers (two of one color and one of another color)

Tapestry needle for weaving in ends and working duplicate stitches and embroidery

GAUGE

With larger needles, approx. 9½ stitches = 2 in. / 5 cm in stranded stockinette stitch, blocked.

Note: If you already know you are a tight knitter (or just want a larger hat), go up one or two needle sizes for both the ribbing and the body of the hat.

With smaller circular needles and color D, cast on 96 stitches. Place single color marker and join in the round, being careful not to twist stitches.

Work (k1 tbl, p1) rib pattern for approximately 1½ to 2 in. / 4 to 5 cm. (tbl=through back loop)

Switch to larger needles and work chart from right to left beginning on Row 1, bottom right corner. Chart repeats three times around the hat.

Use remaining two stitch markers of another color to mark chart repeats.

Note: In order to avoid long "floats" (strands of yarn on the inside of the hat) and to help maintain your tension, do not carry a color more than three or four stitches without twisting the colors around each other in the back of work.

Switch to DPNs when work becomes too small for circular needles.

FINISHING

After chart is complete, cut yarn leaving a 10 in. / 25.5 cm tail. Using a tapestry needle, weave tail through remaining stitches and pull tightly to close circle. Pull tail to inside and weave in all ends.

Block as desired. See page 13 for my favorite hat blocking technique.

After all knitting and blocking is complete, work duplicate stitches in the colors and locations shown on chart.

Optional: Using color F, make French knots for the centers of the peach blossoms in place of duplicate stitching as I did.

KEY

☐ K
Knit

D Dup
Work duplicate stitches after all knitting and blocking is complete.

V S1
Slip one purlwise with yarn in back

/ K2tog
Knit 2 together

■ No Stitch
The "no stitch" squares represent the stitches that were lost due to decreases earlier in the round. *Do not skip a stitch.* Simply treat these squares as if they do not exist.

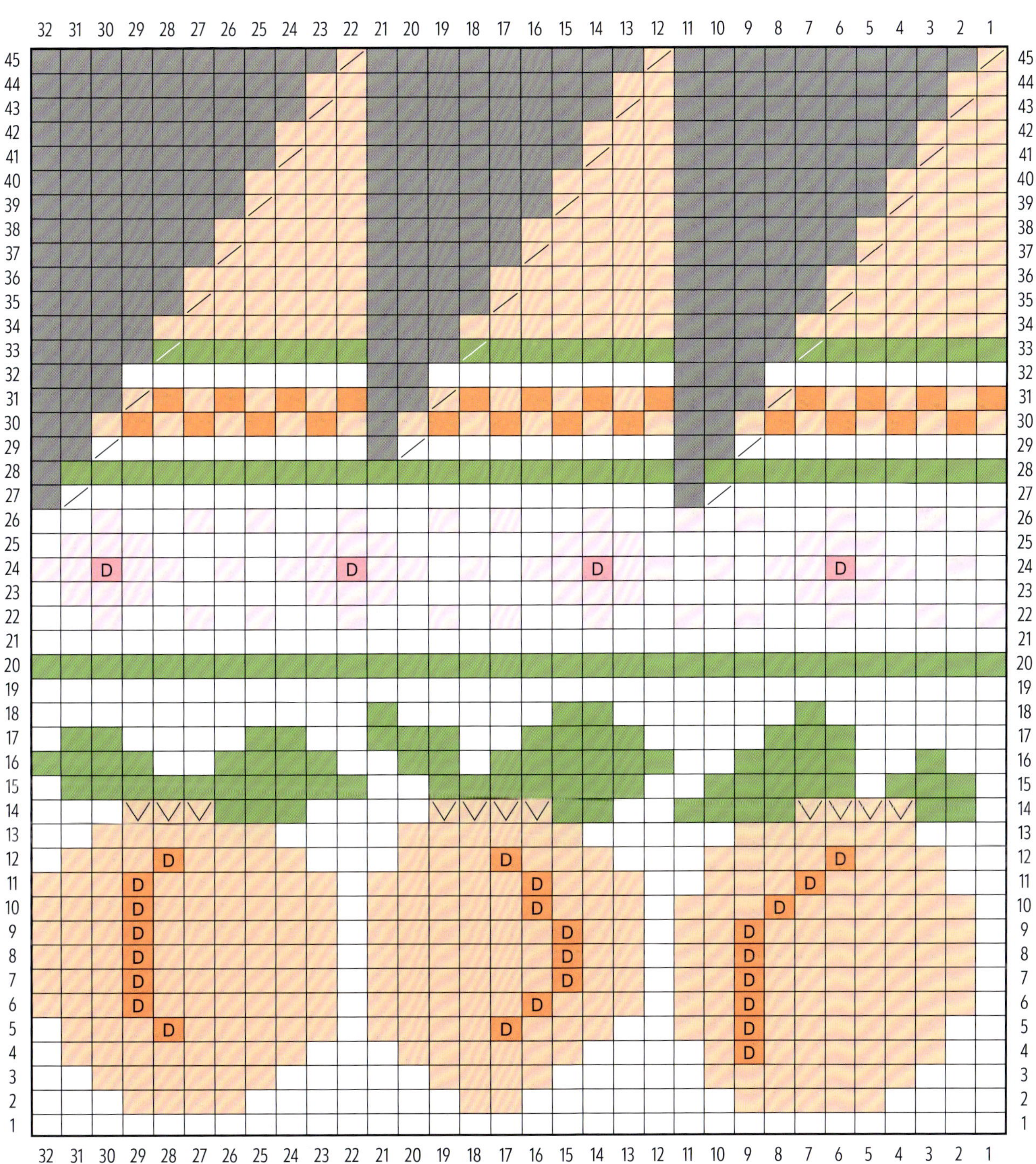

You've probably heard of the Kentucky Derby, Kentucky Fried Chicken, and Louisville Slugger bats. But have you heard of burgoo, moonbows, or hot browns? Unless you're from Kentucky, probably not. You may have also heard of Kentucky's famous bluegrass music, bourbon, actual bluegrass (the grass), Mammoth Cave National Park, or coal fields. But one of the most iconic images of this southeastern state is horses. Gently rolling hills with beautiful horse pastures and black or white fences have become synonymous with Kentucky. The famous Churchill Downs has been hosting the Kentucky Derby since 1875. Oh, and if you're lucky enough to visit this beautiful state, be sure to schedule time to enjoy some burgoo (a meat and vegetable stew) or hot browns (a broiled sandwich topped with Mornay sauce) or watch for moonbows (lunar rainbows) at Cumberland Falls.

Horses in a sun-dappled pasture behind a classic four-rail fence with stables in the background wrap around this design. Add fluffy tails and manes to the horses with fun and simple embroidery.

SIZE

One size fits an average adult size head (approx. 19 in. / 48 cm – 22 in. / 56 cm)

Finished Circumference: approx. 20¼ in. / 51.5 cm.

YARN

Worsted weight yarn (#4) in eight colors. Shown in:

- **A:** Stunning String Studio Legacy Worsted: Autumn Sage (33 g / 71 yd. / 65 m)
- **B:** Aly Bee Workshop Merino Worsted: Natural (15 g / 30 yd. / 27 m)
- **C:** Malabrigo Rios: Lettuce (10 g / 21 yd. / 19 m)
- **D:** Stunning String Studio Legacy Worsted: Deep Forest (15 g / 32 yd. / 29 m)
- **E:** Aly Bee Workshop Merino Worsted: Buttered Popcorn (5 g / 10 yd. / 9 m)
- **F:** Aly Bee Workshop Merino Worsted: Glass Slipper (20 g / 40 yd. / 37 m)
- **G:** *Malabrigo Rios: Cape Cod Gray (Approx. 6 yd. / 5 m)
- **H:** *Aly Bee Workshop Merino Worsted: Farmhouse (Approx. 12 yd. / 11 m)

*Used only in duplicate stitching

Continued on next page

NEEDLES

- US size 5 / 3.75 mm, 16 in. / 40 cm circular knitting needles
- US size 7 / 4.5 mm, 16 in. / 40 cm circular knitting needles
- US size 7 / 4.5 mm, set of double-pointed needles (DPNs)
- (or size needed to obtain gauge)

NOTIONS

3 stitch markers (two of one color and one of another color)

Tapestry needle for weaving in ends and working duplicate stitches and embroidery

GAUGE

With larger needles, approx. 9½ stitches = 2 in. / 5 cm in stranded stockinette stitch, blocked.

Note: If you already know you are a tight knitter (or just want a larger hat), go up one or two needle sizes for both the ribbing and the body of the hat.

With smaller circular needles and color A, cast on 96 stitches. Place single color marker and join in the round, being careful not to twist stitches.

Work (k1, p1) rib pattern for approximately 1½ to 2 in. / 4 to 5 cm.

Switch to larger needles and work chart from right to left beginning on Row 1, bottom right corner. Chart repeats three times around the hat. Use remaining two stitch markers of another color to mark chart repeats.

Note: In order to avoid long "floats" (strands of yarn on the inside of the hat) and to help maintain your tension, do not carry a color more than three or four stitches without twisting the colors around each other in the back of work.

Switch to DPNs when work becomes too small for circular needles.

FINISHING

After chart is complete, cut yarn leaving a 10 in. / 25.5 cm tail. Using a tapestry needle, weave tail through remaining stitches and pull tightly to close circle. Pull tail to inside and weave in all ends.

Block as desired. See page 13 for my favorite hat blocking technique.

Duplicate stitching and embroidery: After all blocking is complete, work all duplicate stitches in the colors and locations shown on chart. For a varied look, try using different colors for the horses. Using any color desired, add tails and manes to horses using small straight stitches. You may need to separate the yarn and use only 2 plies if it seems too thick. For the tails, I left the ends of the yarn free and then separated the plies. See photos for inspiration.

KEY

- ☐ K — Knit
- D Dup — Work duplicate stitches after all knitting and blocking is complete.
- ╱ K2tog — Knit 2 together
- ■ No Stitch — The "no stitch" squares represent the stitches that were lost due to decreases earlier in the round. *Do not skip a stitch.* Simply treat these squares as if they do not exist.
- V S1 — Slip one purlwise with yarn in back

32 31 30 29 28 27 26 25 24 23 22 21 20 19 18 17 16 15 14 13 12 11 10 9 8 7 6 5 4 3 2 1
45 44 43 42 41 40 39 38 37 36 35 34 33 32 31 30 29 28 27 26 25 24 23 22 21 20 19 18 17 16 15 14 13 12 11 10 9 8 7 6 5 4 3 2 1

What words come to mind when you think of Louisiana? *Cajun*, *gumbo*, *Creole*, *bayous*, *jambalaya*, *African*, *crawfish*, *Spanish*, *beignets*, *French*, *jazz*, *Mardi Gras*—likely a *long* and colorful list of words representing the cuisine, cultures, and celebrations that make Louisiana unique. The rich, bold flavors found in restaurants and homes around the state come from a history of blended cultures and a passion for using local ingredients. Even the architecture of homes and businesses reveals a unique fusion of cultural influences, from tiny bungalows to lavish houses.

This design takes you to the French Quarter of New Orleans where wrought iron railings and fences are commonplace. The intricate wrought iron design is followed by a classic Mardi Gras–inspired motif in rich yet subdued colors. The diamond patterns in the design create a flower on the crown of the hat reminiscent of the yellow coneflowers found throughout the state.

SIZE

One size fits an average adult size head (approx. 19 in. / 48 cm – 22 in. / 56 cm)

Finished Circumference approx. 20¼ in. / 51.5 cm.

YARN

Worsted weight yarn (#4) in five colors. Shown in:

- **A:** Aly Bee Workshop Merino Worsted: Spooky (41 g / 83 yd. / 76 m)
- **B:** Aly Bee Workshop Merino Worsted: Rainy Day (15 g / 30 yd. / 27 m)
- **C:** Stunning String Studio Legacy Worsted: Spicy Mustard (25 g / 54 yd. / 49 m)
- **D:** Stunning String Studio Legacy Worsted: Black Forest (15 g / 32 yd. / 29 m)
- **E:** Malabrigo Rios: Sabiduria (10 g / 21 yd. / 19 m)

Continued on next page

NEEDLES

- US size 5 / 3.75 mm, 16 in. / 40 cm circular knitting needles
- US size 7 / 4.5 mm, 16 in. / 40 cm circular knitting needles
- US size 7 / 4.5 mm, set of double-pointed needles (DPNs)
- (or size needed to obtain gauge)

NOTIONS

3 stitch markers (two of one color and one of another color)

Tapestry needle for weaving in ends and working duplicate stitches

GAUGE

With larger needles, approx. 9½ stitches = 2 in. / 5 cm in stranded stockinette stitch, blocked.

Note: If you already know you are a tight knitter (or just want a larger hat), go up one or two needle sizes for both the ribbing and the body of the hat.

With smaller circular needles and color A, cast on 96 stitches. Place single color marker and join in the round, being careful not to twist stitches.

Work (k2, p2) rib pattern for approximately 1½ to 2 in. / 4 to 5 cm.

Increase Round: *K31, kfb; repeat from * 2 more times - 99 sts total.

Switch to larger needles and work chart from right to left beginning on Row 1, bottom right corner. Chart repeats three times around the hat. Use remaining two stitch markers of another color to mark chart repeats.

Note: In order to avoid long "floats" (strands of yarn on the inside of the hat) and to help maintain your tension, do not carry a color more than three or four stitches without twisting the colors around each other in the back of work.

Special instructions: At the end of Row 41, remove marker, slip 1 stitch to right needle, replace marker. The 2 "chart repeat markers" on Row 42 will also need to be moved as described. Work Row 42 and remainder of chart as shown.

Switch to DPNs when work becomes too small for circular needles.

FINISHING

After chart is complete, cut yarn leaving a 10 in. / 25.5 cm tail.

Using a tapestry needle, weave tail through remaining stitches and pull tightly to close circle. Pull tail to inside and weave in all ends.

Block as desired. See page 13 for my favorite hat blocking technique.

After all blocking is complete, work duplicate stitches where shown using color A.

KEY

- ☐ K — Knit
- [D] Dup — Work duplicate stitches after all knitting and blocking is complete.
- [/] K2tog — Knit 2 together
- ■ No Stitch — The "no stitch" squares represent the stitches that were lost due to decreases earlier in the round. *Do not skip a stitch.* Simply treat these squares as if they do not exist.

Note: ★ At the end of Row 41, remove marker, slip 1 stitch to right needle, replace marker. The 2 "chart repeat markers" on Row 42 will also need to be moved as described.

Work Row 42 and remainder of chart as shown.

The Mississippi River and the people who live near it have been intrinsically linked since humans first roamed the land. For Mississippians today, the river is a vital resource for transportation, industry, and tourism—and it holds a rich history. It's hard to even think about Mississippi without picturing a vintage paddle-wheel boat on the river. This diverse state is filled with historical sites, outdoor adventure opportunities, agriculture, unique regional cuisine, and music, specifically gospel, Delta blues, and jazz. History buffs can explore the famous Mississippi Civil Rights Museum and Vicksburg National Military Park while a peaceful drive along the historic Natchez Trace Parkway might be just the thing for someone else. Without a doubt, Mississippi wins for having the most fun and rhythmic name, especially when spelling it aloud!

Magnolias, the large fragrant flowers that hold the title of state flower and inspire the state nickname, are the focal point of this design with blooms and buds alongside the muddy Mississippi River.

SIZE

One size fits an average adult size head (approx. 19 in. / 48 cm – 22 in. / 56 cm)

Finished Circumference approx. 20¼ in. / 51.5 cm.

YARN

Worsted weight yarn (#4) in five colors. Shown in:

- **A:** Dragonfly Fibers Sylph Worsted: Saugerties (48 g/ 84 yd./ 77 m)
- **B:** Stunning String Studio Legacy Worsted: Deep Forest (25 g / 54 yd. / 49 m)
- **C:** Malabrigo Rios: Natural (10 g / 21 yd. / 19 m)
- **D:** *Aly Bee Workshop Merino Worsted: Honeybee (5 g / 10 yd. / 9 m)
- **E:** Fiber Seed Sprout Worsted: Fawn (15 g / 28 yd. / 26 m)

*Used only in duplicate stitching and French knots

Continued on next page

NEEDLES

- US size 5 / 3.75 mm, 16 in. / 40 cm circular knitting needles
- US size 7 / 4.5 mm, 16 in. / 40 cm circular knitting needles
- US size 7 / 4.5 mm, set of double-pointed needles (DPNs)
- (or size needed to obtain gauge)

NOTIONS

3 stitch markers (two of one color and one of another color)

Tapestry needle for weaving in ends and working duplicate stitches and embroidery

GAUGE

With larger needles, approx. 9½ stitches = 2 in. / 5 cm in stranded stockinette stitch, blocked.

Note: If you already know you are a tight knitter (or just want a larger hat), go up one or two needle sizes for both the ribbing and the body of the hat.

With smaller circular needles and color B cast on 96 stitches. Place single color marker and join in the round, being careful not to twist stitches.

Work (k1, p1) rib pattern for approximately 1½ to 2 in. / 4 to 5 cm.

Increase Round: *K31, kfb; repeat from * 2 more times - 99 sts total.

Switch to larger needles and work chart from right to left beginning on Row 1, bottom right corner. Chart repeats three times around the hat. Use remaining two stitch markers of another color to mark chart repeats.

Note: In order to avoid long "floats" (strands of yarn on the inside of the hat) and to help maintain your tension, do not carry a color more than three or four stitches without twisting the colors around each other in the back of work.

Switch to DPNs when work becomes too small for circular needles.

FINISHING

After chart is complete, cut yarn leaving a 10 in. / 25.5 cm tail. Using a tapestry needle, weave tail through remaining stitches and pull tightly to close circle. Pull tail to inside and weave in all ends.

Block as desired. See page 13 for my favorite hat blocking technique.

After all knitting and blocking is complete, work duplicate stitches in the colors and locations shown. Add French knots to flower bud centers where shown using a tapestry needle and color D.

KEY

☐ K
Knit

D Dup
Work duplicate stitches after all knitting and blocking is complete.

F French Knot
Add French knots where shown after all knitting and blocking is complete

V S1
Slip one purlwise with yarn in back

/ K2tog
Knit 2 together

■ No Stitch
The "no stitch" squares represent the stitches that were lost due to decreases earlier in the round. *Do not skip a stitch*. Simply treat these squares as if they do not exist.

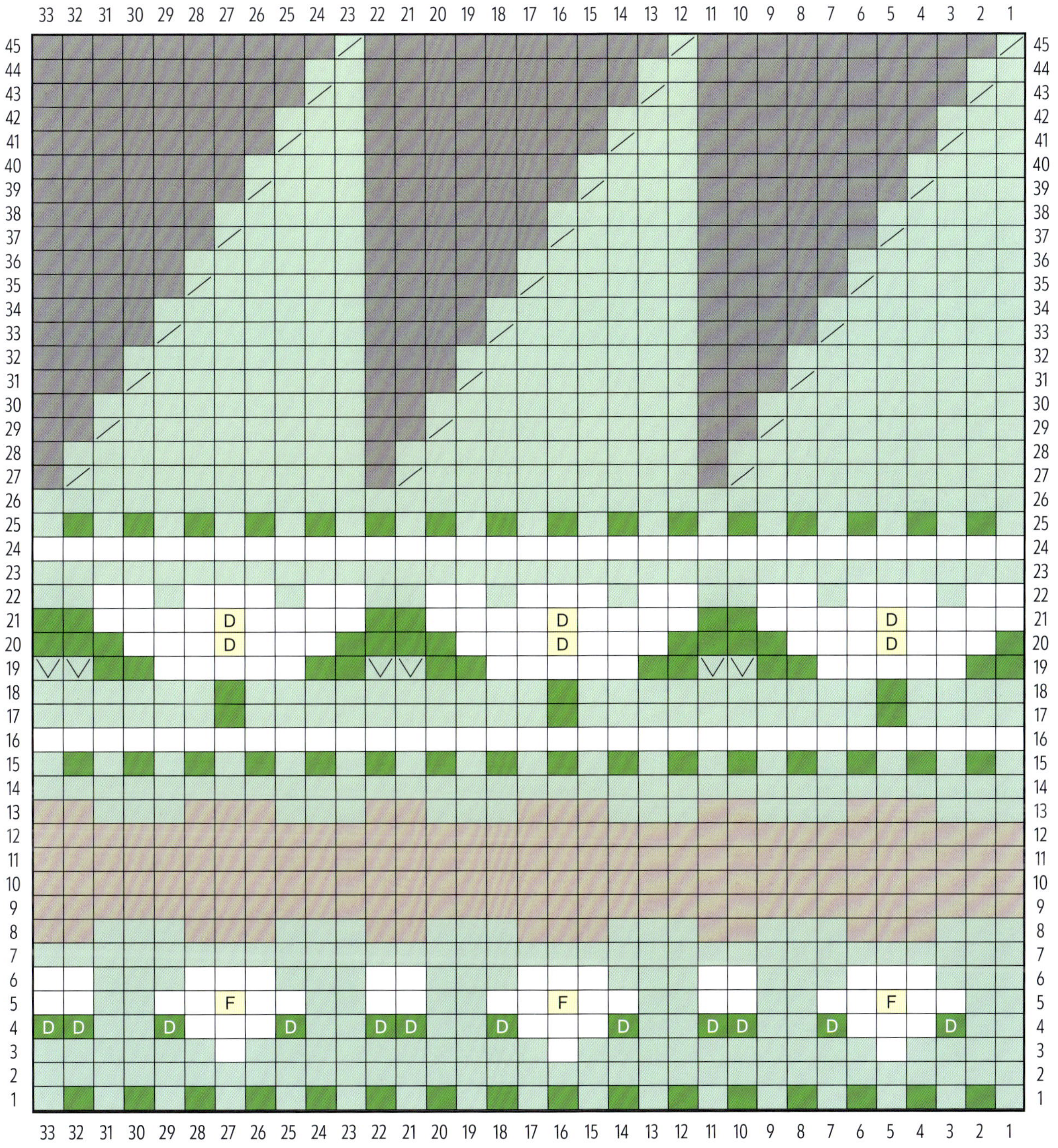

The fact that carnivorous plants even exist is pretty fascinating, but the fact that *more than half* of the known species of carnivorous plants are native to North Carolina and can be found growing in the wild is absolutely incredible! The "just right" combination of sand, water, sunlight, and low-nutrient soil found in many parts of the state creates the unique environment for these unusual plants, which supplement nutrients with insects, to thrive.

This fun-to-knit design features pitcher plants and Venus flytraps growing in a cross section of soil, exposing shallow and deep roots. Additional embroidery adds texture and dimension. Just for fun, insect-shaped buttons bring the scene to life.

SIZE

One size fits an average adult size head (approx. 19 in. / 48 cm – 22 in. / 56 cm)

Finished Circumference: approx. 20¼ in. / 51.5 cm.

YARN

Worsted weight yarn (#4) in six colors. Shown in:

- **A:** Malabrigo Rios: Coco (25 g / 53 yd. / 48 m)
- **B:** Stunning String Studio Legacy Worsted: Dried Hops (5 g / 11 yd. / 10 m)
- **C:** Malabrigo Rios: Lettuce (25 g / 53 yd. / 48 m)
- **D:** Stunning String Studio Legacy Worsted: Stone (33 g / 71 yd. / 65 m)
- **E:** *Stunning String Studio Legacy Worsted: Sandalwood (Approx. 6 yd. / 5 m)
- **F:** Stunning String Studio Legacy Worsted: Yellow Pear (10g / 21 yd. / 19 m)

*Used only in duplicate stitching

Continued on next page

NEEDLES

- US size 5 / 3.75 mm, 16 in. / 40 cm circular knitting needles
- US size 7 / 4.5 mm, 16 in. / 40 cm circular knitting needles
- US size 7 / 4.5 mm, set of double-pointed needles (DPNs)
- (or size needed to obtain gauge)

NOTIONS

3 stitch markers (two of one color and one of another color)

Tapestry needle for weaving in ends and working duplicate stitches and embroidery

GAUGE

With larger needles, approx. 9½ stitches = 2 in. / 5 cm in stranded stockinette stitch, blocked.

Note: If you already know you are a tight knitter (or just want a larger hat), go up one or two needle sizes for both the ribbing and the body of the hat.

With smaller circular needles and color A, cast on 96 stitches. Place single color marker and join in the round, being careful not to twist stitches.

Work (k1 tbl, p1) rib pattern for approximately 1½ to 2 in. / 4 to 5 cm.
(tbl=through back loop)

Switch to larger needles and work chart from right to left beginning on Row 1, bottom right corner. Chart repeats three times around the hat.

Use remaining two stitch markers of another color to mark chart repeats.

Note: In order to avoid long "floats" (strands of yarn on the inside of the hat) and to help maintain your tension, do not carry a color more than three or four stitches without twisting the colors around each other in the back of work.

Switch to DPNs when work becomes too small for circular needles.

FINISHING

After chart is complete, cut yarn leaving a 10 in. / 25.5 cm tail. Using a tapestry needle, weave tail through remaining stitches and pull tightly to close circle. Pull tail to inside and weave in all ends.

Block as desired. See page 13 for my favorite hat blocking technique.

After all blocking is complete, work all duplicate stitches in the colors and locations shown on chart. Using straight stitches, add "teeth" to the Venus Fly Traps with color F and additional roots with color B. I separated the 4 plies of yarn and used only 2 plies for these stitches. See photo for inspiration. Attach or embroider flies as desired.

KEY

☐ **K**
Knit

D **Dup**
Work duplicate stitches after all knitting and blocking is complete.

⁄ **K2tog**
Knit 2 together

■ **No Stitch**
The "no stitch" squares represent the stitches that were lost due to decreases earlier in the round. *Do not skip a stitch.* Simply treat these squares as if they do not exist.

V **S1**
Slip one purlwise with yarn in back

One of the best (and tastiest) parts of visiting other states is sampling the regional cuisine. From famous Myrtle Beach and the historic city of Charleston to lush rolling hills and the Blue Ridge Mountains, South Carolinians take a great deal of pride in their local dishes—served with a side of Southern hospitality, of course. Ingredients such as grits, shrimp, rice, collard greens, chicken, and oysters are synonymous with South Carolina cuisine and Southern cooking as a whole. And of course, there's the unforgettable and tangy South Carolina barbecue, the official state picnic cuisine, best served with a tall glass of sweet tea. And no trip to the state is complete without picking up a bag of boiled peanuts from a roadside stand.

This design features Frogmore stew, a South Carolina seafood boil made with shrimp, corn on the cob, and potato slices cooked in beer with spices. This local favorite was traditionally served on layers of newspaper.

SIZE

One size fits an average adult size head (approx. 19 in. / 48 cm – 22 in. / 56 cm)

Finished Circumference: approx. 20¼ in. / 51.5 cm.

YARN

Worsted weight yarn (#4) in eight colors. Shown in:

- **A:** Not shown on chart. Dragonfly Fibers Sylph Worsted: Birch (24 g/ 42 yd./ 38 m)
- **B:** Aly Bee Workshop Merino Worsted: Mead (15 g / 30 yd. / 27 m)
- **C:** Aly Bee Workshop Merino Worsted: Maple Leaf (15 g / 30 yd. / 27 m)
- **D:** Stunning String Studio Legacy Worsted: Fading Sunlight (15 g / 32 yd. / 29 m)
- **E:** Aly Bee Workshop Merino Worsted: Farmhouse (20 g / 40 yd. / 36 m)
- **F:** Aly Bee Workshop Merino Worsted: Moscato (10 g / 20 yd. / 18 m)
- **G:** Stunning String Studio Legacy Worsted: Oregon Trail (10 g / 21 yd. / 19 m)
- **H:** Aly Bee Workshop Merino Worsted: Kettle Corn (5 g / 10 yd. / 9 m)

Continued on next page

NEEDLES

- US size 5 / 3.75 mm, 16 in. / 40 cm circular knitting needles
- US size 7 / 4.5 mm, 16 in. / 40 cm circular knitting needles
- US size 7 / 4.5 mm, set of double-pointed needles (DPNs)
- (or size needed to obtain gauge)

NOTIONS

3 stitch markers (two of one color and one of another color)

Tapestry needle for weaving in ends and working duplicate stitches

GAUGE

With larger needles, approx. 9½ stitches = 2 in. / 5 cm in stranded stockinette stitch, blocked.

Note: If you already know you are a tight knitter (or just want a larger hat), go up one or two needle sizes for both the ribbing and the body of the hat.

With smaller circular needles and color A, cast on 96 stitches. Place single color marker and join in the round, being careful not to twist stitches.

Work (k2, p2) rib pattern for approximately 1½ to 2 in. / 4 to 5 cm.

Switch to larger needles and work chart from right to left beginning on Row 1, bottom right corner. Chart repeats three times around the hat. Use remaining two stitch markers of another color to mark chart repeats.

Note: In order to avoid long "floats" (strands of yarn on the inside of the hat) and to help maintain your tension, do not carry a color more than three or four stitches without twisting the colors around each other in the back of work.

Switch to DPNs when work becomes too small for circular needles.

FINISHING

After chart is complete, cut yarn leaving a 10 in. / 25.5 cm tail. Using a tapestry needle, weave tail through remaining stitches and pull tightly to close circle. Pull tail to inside and weave in all ends.

Block as desired. See page 13 for my favorite hat blocking technique.

After all blocking is complete, work duplicate stitches between the potato slices using a tapestry needle and color B.

KEY

☐ K
Knit

⊡ P
Purl

D Dup
Work duplicate stitches after all knitting and blocking is complete.

⧄ K2tog
Knit 2 together

■ No Stitch
The "no stitch" squares represent the stitches that were lost due to decreases earlier in the round. *Do not skip a stitch*. Simply treat these squares as if they do not exist.

From country and bluegrass to rock and roll and the blues, musical roots run deep in Tennessee. The state capital (and country music capital of the world), Nashville, is home to the Country Music Hall of Fame as well as the Grand Ole Opry, the longest running US radio show, where country music legends share the stage with aspiring newcomers. Even the King of Rock and Roll himself, Elvis, called Tennessee home at his famous Graceland estate.

In this design, soothing colors and the images of a piano, guitar, banjo, vintage microphone, and musical staff celebrate the music that has become synonymous with Tennessee and the people who live there.

SIZE

One size fits an average adult size head (approx. 19 in. / 48 cm – 22 in. / 56 cm)

Finished Circumference: approx. 20¼ in. / 51.5 cm.

YARN

Worsted weight yarn (#4) in five colors. Shown in:

- **A:** *Malabrigo Rios: Natural, not shown on chart (15 g / 32 yd. / 29 m)
- **B:** *Malabrigo Rios: Black, not shown on chart (10 g / 21 yd. / 19 m)
- **C:** Malabrigo Rios: Denim (40 g / 84 yd. / 77 m)
- **D:** Aly Bee Workshop Merino Worsted: Sourdough (20 g / 40 yd. / 37 m)
- **E:** Aly Bee Workshop Merino Worsted: Raspberry Ice (15 g / 30 yd. / 27 m)

*Used only in piano rib pattern

Approximately 5–8 yards each of any brown and silver yarn for the duplicate stitching on the instruments and microphone.

Continued on next page

NEEDLES

- US size 5 / 3.75 mm, 16 in. / 40 cm circular knitting needles
- US size 7 / 4.5 mm, 16 in. / 40 cm circular knitting needles
- US size 7 / 4.5 mm, set of double-pointed needles (DPNs)
- (or size needed to obtain gauge)

NOTIONS

3 stitch markers (two of one color and one of another color)

Tapestry needle for weaving in ends and working duplicate stitches and embroidery

Buttons or beads for the music notes (optional)

Embroidery needle and floss to attach beads (optional)

GAUGE

With larger needles, approx. 9½ stitches = 2 in. / 5 cm in stranded stockinette stitch, blocked.

Note: If you already know you are a tight knitter (or just want a larger hat), go up one or two needle sizes for both the ribbing and the body of the hat.

With smaller circular needles and color A, cast on 96 stitches. Place single color marker and join in the round, being careful not to twist stitches.

Piano Key Ribbing:
Work 2 rounds of (k1, p1) rib pattern in color A.

Work the Piano (k1, p1) rib pattern (chart at top of p. 101) for another 8 rows using colors A and B (natural and black) as shown.

Work chart from right to left, repeating to end of round.

Note: when you reach the last repeat in the round, you will only have room for 1 black piano key instead of 2 at the end of the pattern. This will make more sense when you get there.

Switch to larger needles and work chart from right to left beginning on Row 1, bottom right corner. Chart repeats three times around the hat. Use remaining two stitch markers of another color to mark chart repeats.

Note: In order to avoid long "floats" (strands of yarn on the inside of the hat) and to help maintain your tension, do not carry a color more than three or four stitches without twisting the colors around each other in the back of work.

Switch to DPNs when work becomes too small for circular needles.

FINISHING

After chart is complete, cut yarn leaving a 10 in. / 25.5 cm tail. Using a tapestry needle, weave tail through remaining stitches and pull tightly to close circle. Pull tail to inside and weave in all ends.

Block as desired. See page 13 for my favorite hat blocking technique.

Embellishments: After all knitting and blocking is complete, add duplicate stitching where shown on the instruments and microphone using the brown and silver yarns. See notes under chart for tips.

Optional: Use simple straight stitches to add "sound lines" around microphone and music notes on staff. See photos for inspiration. The notes can be completed with French knots, beads, or buttons. I used buttons and sewed them on with embroidery floss.

KEY

☐	K Knit
D	Dup Work duplicate stitches after all knitting and blocking is complete.
╱	K2tog Knit 2 together
■	No Stitch The "no stitch" squares represent the stitches that were lost due to decreases earlier in the round. *Do not skip a stitch.* Simply treat these squares as if they do not exist.

Piano rib pattern

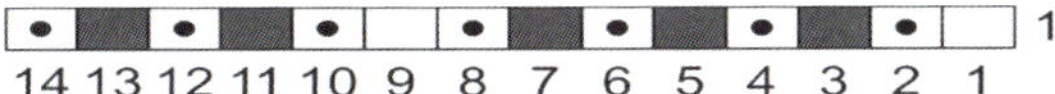

Microphone stand rows 4-11: Knit with color D and duplicate stitch with silver.

Microphone stand, banjo, and guitar rows 13-22: Knit with color C or E as makes sense and duplicate stitch with colors shown

All duplicate stitches in rows 23-25: Knit with color D and duplicate stitch with colors shown.

ASCEND

A visit to Virginia means different things to different people. It could mean a visual and interactive journey through history, an exhilarating hike along the Appalachian Trail, a scenic drive through the mountains, a cave exploration, a solemn stroll through a national cemetery, or even a bike ride to look for wild ponies. So many choices! Maybe that's why "Virginia is for Lovers"... because there's something for everybody to love! The best part is that you can easily do it all. Because of the not-too-large size of Virginia, driving from historical sites or life-size dinosaur sculptures to wineries or epic camping is never more than a day's drive away. Perfect for road trip adventures!

In this design, lush rolling hills and farmlands (with a classic Virginia split rail fence in the foreground) are just a sampling of what this beautiful and history-filled state has to offer.

SIZE

One size fits an average adult size head (approx. 19 in. / 48 cm – 22 in. / 56 cm)

Finished Circumference: approx. 20¼ in. / 51.5 cm.

YARN

Worsted weight yarn (#4) in five colors. Shown in:

- **A:** Polka Dot Sheep Whitefish Worsted: Barnwood (10 g / 21 yd. / 19 m)
- **B:** Stunning String Legacy Worsted: Black Forest (33 g / 71 yd. / 65 m)
- **C:** Malabrigo Rios: Lettuce (20 g / 42 yd. / 38 m)
- **D:** Stunning String Legacy Worsted: Fern Grotto (20 g/ 43 yd. / 39 m)
- **E:** Malabrigo Rios: Cosmos (15 g / 32 yd. / 29 m)

NEEDLES

- US size 5 / 3.75 mm, 16 in. / 40 cm circular knitting needles
- US size 7 / 4.5 mm, 16 in. / 40 cm circular knitting needles
- US size 7 / 4.5 mm, set of double-pointed needles (DPNs)
- (or size needed to obtain gauge)

Continued on next page

NOTIONS

3 stitch markers (two of one color and one of another color)

Tapestry needle for weaving in ends and working optional duplicate stitching on fence

GAUGE

With larger needles, approx. 9½ stitches = 2 in. / 5 cm in stranded stockinette stitch, blocked.

Note: If you already know you are a tight knitter (or just want a larger hat), go up one or two needle sizes for both the ribbing and the body of the hat.

With smaller circular needles and color B, cast on 96 stitches. Place single color marker and join in the round, being careful not to twist stitches.

Work (k1 tbl, 1) rib pattern for approximately 1½ to 2 in. / 4 to 5 cm. (tbl=through back loop)

Switch to larger needles and work chart from right to left beginning on Row 1, bottom right corner. Chart repeats three times around the hat. Use remaining two stitch markers of another color to mark chart repeats.

Note: In order to avoid long "floats" (strands of yarn on the inside of the hat) and to help maintain your tension, do not carry a color more than three or four stitches without twisting the colors around each other in the back of work.

Switch to DPNs when work becomes too small for circular needles.

FINISHING

After chart is complete, cut yarn leaving a 10 in. / 25.5 cm tail. Using a tapestry needle, weave tail through remaining stitches and pull tightly to close circle. Pull tail to inside and weave in all ends.

Block as desired. See page 13 for my favorite hat blocking technique.

Optional: After the blocking was complete, I duplicate stitched over the entire fence using color A just to make it stand out more.

KEY

- ☐ K — Knit
- ☑ S1 — Slip one purlwise with yarn in back
- ⧄ K2tog — Knit 2 together
- ■ No Stitch — The "no stitch" squares represent the stitches that were lost due to decreases earlier in the round. *Do not skip a stitch.* Simply treat these squares as if they do not exist.

"Almost heaven, West Virginia." John Denver's lyrics perfectly capture the beautiful landscape of the Mountain State, the only state located completely within the Appalachian Mountains. As such, spectacular forests, waterfalls, meadows, rivers, streams, and an abundance of wildlife can be found across the state and around every corner. Country roads take you to small towns rich in Appalachian culture, coal mining history, and country charm where even the drive itself is a treasure. Adventure-seeking visitors and locals alike are drawn to New River Gorge National Park and Preserve and dozens of beautiful state parks for adventures of all types in all seasons. No matter where you choose to go or which direction you turn in this scenic state, you're going to want to stay awhile.

This design features a wildflower-filled meadow and a lush forest against a backdrop of the Blue Ridge Mountains.

SIZE

One size fits an average adult size head (approx. 19 in. / 48 cm – 22 in. / 56 cm)

Finished Circumference: approx. 20¼ in. / 51.5 cm.

YARN

Worsted weight yarn (#4) in seven colors. Shown in:

- **A:** Malabrigo Rios: Ivy (33 g / 69 yd. / 63 m)
- **B:** Malabrigo Rios: Natural (5 g / 11 yd. / 10 m))
- **C:** Stunning String Studio Legacy Worsted: Goldenrod (5 g / 11 yd. / 10 m)
- **D:** Stunning String Studio Legacy Worsted: Deep Forest (20 g / 43yd. / 39 m)
- **E:** Malabrigo Rios: Bobby Blue (15 g / 32 yd. / 29 m)
- **F:** Peekaboo Yarns Merino Worsted: Zion Blue (15 g / 33 yd. / 30 m)
- **G:** Malabrigo Rios: Cosmos (10 g / 21 yd. / 19 m)

Continued on next page

NEEDLES

- US size 5 / 3.75 mm, 16 in. / 40 cm circular knitting needles
- US size 7 / 4.5 mm, 16 in. / 40 cm circular knitting needles
- US size 7 / 4.5 mm, set of double-pointed needles (DPNs)
- (or size needed to obtain gauge)

NOTIONS

3 stitch markers (two of one color and one of another color)

Tapestry needle for weaving in ends and working duplicate stitches

GAUGE

With larger needles, approx. 9½ stitches = 2 in. / 5 cm in stranded stockinette stitch, blocked.

Note: If you already know you are a tight knitter (or just want a larger hat), go up one or two needle sizes for both the ribbing and the body of the hat.

With smaller circular needles and color A, cast on 96 stitches. Place single color marker and join in the round, being careful not to twist stitches.

Work (k1, p1) rib pattern for approximately 1½ to 2 in. / 4 to 5 cm.

Switch to larger needles and work chart from right to left beginning on Row 1, bottom right corner. Chart repeats three times around the hat. Use remaining two stitch markers of another color to mark chart repeats.

Note: In order to avoid long "floats" (strands of yarn on the inside of the hat) and to help maintain your tension, do not carry a color more than three or four stitches without twisting the colors around each other in the back of work.

Switch to DPNs when work becomes too small for circular needles.

FINISHING

After chart is complete, cut yarn leaving a 10 in. / 25.5 cm tail. Using a tapestry needle, weave tail through remaining stitches and pull tightly to close circle. Pull tail to inside and weave in all ends.

Block as desired. See page 13 for my favorite hat blocking technique.

Duplicate stitching:

After all blocking is complete, work duplicate stitches where shown using color C to add centers to flowers.

KEY

☐ K
Knit

D Dup
Work duplicate stitches after all knitting and blocking is complete.

V S1
Slip one purlwise with yarn in back

/ K2tog
Knit 2 together

■ No Stitch
The "no stitch" squares represent the stitches that were lost due to decreases earlier in the round. *Do not skip a stitch.* Simply treat these squares as if they do not exist.

THE MIDWEST

Illinois

Indiana

Iowa

Kansas

Michigan

Minnesota

Missouri

Nebraska

North Dakota

Ohio

South Dakota

Wisconsin

Nicknamed the Land of Lincoln, Illinois is also known for vast farmlands, delicious pizza and hot dogs, and a rich and diverse art scene embracing all mediums, including stained glass. From the world's largest Tiffany stained-glass dome at the Chicago Cultural Center to the dome of the capitol building in Springfield to numerous churches, chapels, museums, and private homes throughout the state, stained glass has become a beloved art form for generations of Illinoisans.

In this colorful interpretation of stained glass, simple images represent the heart of the state from agriculture (pumpkins and corn) and state symbols (violets and white oak leaves) to Mr. Abraham Lincoln himself.

SIZE

One size fits an average adult size head (approx. 19 in. / 48 cm – 22 in. / 56 cm)

Finished Circumference: approx. 20¼ in. / 51.5 cm.

YARN

Worsted weight yarn (#4) in six colors. Shown in:

- **A:** Schmutzerella Yarns Epic: I Want to Be a Bellhop (25 g / 54 yd. / 49 m)
- **B:** Malabrigo Rios: Black (33 g / 69 yd. / 63 m)
- **C:** Aly Bee Workshop Merino Worsted: Honeybee (20 g / 40 yd. / 37 m)
- **D:** Polka Dot Sheep Whitefish Worsted: Helena (15 g / 32 yd. / 29 m)
- **E:** Malabrigo Rios: Cian (10 g / 21 yd. / 19 m)
- **F:** Malabrigo Rios: Matisse Blue (10 g / 21 yd. / 19m)

Continued on next page

NEEDLES

- US size 5 / 3.75 mm, 16 in. / 40 cm circular knitting needles
- US size 7 / 4.5 mm, 16 in. / 40 cm circular knitting needles
- US size 7 / 4.5 mm, set of double-pointed needles (DPNs)
- (or size needed to obtain gauge)

NOTIONS

3 stitch markers (two of one color and one of another color)

Tapestry needle for weaving in ends and working embroidery

GAUGE

With larger needles, approx. 9½ stitches = 2 in. / 5 cm in stranded stockinette stitch, blocked.

Note: If you already know you are a tight knitter (or just want a larger hat), go up one or two needle sizes for both the ribbing and the body of the hat.

With smaller circular needles and color A, cast on 96 stitches. Place single color marker and join in the round, being careful not to twist stitches.

Work (k1, p1) rib pattern for approximately 1½ to 2 in. / 4 to 5 cm.

Switch to larger needles and work chart from right to left beginning on Row 1, bottom right corner. Chart repeats three times around the hat. Use remaining two stitch markers of another color to mark chart repeats.

Switch to DPNs when work becomes too small for circular needles.

FINISHING

After chart is complete, cut yarn leaving a 10 in. / 25.5 cm tail. Using a tapestry needle, weave tail through remaining stitches and pull tightly to close circle. Pull tail to inside and weave in all ends.

Block as desired. See page 13 for my favorite hat blocking technique.

Optional: Using tapestry needle and color B, add additional black patinaed "lead lines" to all or some of the glass panels to give it even more of the stained-glass look. I also added lines to the pumpkins. See photo for inspiration.

KEY

☐ K
Knit

⧄ K2tog
Knit 2 together

■ No Stitch
The "no stitch" squares represent the stitches that were lost due to decreases earlier in the round. *Do not skip a stitch*. Simply treat these squares as if they do not exist.

Famous for the Indianapolis 500 and Indiana Dunes National Park, this Midwest state also boasts twenty-four state parks with beauty that changes with the seasons, a population with a deep passion for basketball and racing, and a rich farming industry. You'll also find dozens of museums in Indiana that run the gamut from art, superheroes, and cars to Native American culture, dinosaurs, medical history, and the Underground Railroad. But there's also something about Indiana that has a hometown vibe to it. Amid and between the vast farmlands and major cities are hundreds of small towns and communities, some of which are found on "Best Small Towns in America" lists year after year. The charming small town of Santa Claus receives (and responds to) thousands of letters to Santa each year. What a great example of hometown pride!

Featuring peonies (the state flower) and a vintage color palette, this design embraces that small town vibe with a unique pattern one might find on handmade cushions or wallpaper in neighborhood homes and farmhouses.

SIZE

One size fits an average adult size head (approx. 19 in. / 48 cm – 22 in. / 56 cm)

Finished Circumference: approx. 20¼ in. / 51.5 cm.

YARN

Worsted weight yarn (#4) in five colors. Shown in:

- **A:** Polka Dot Sheep Whitefish Worsted: Starfish (40 g / 87 yd. / 80 m)
- **B:** Malabrigo Rios: Ivory (33 g / 69 yd. / 63 m)
- **C:** *Polka Dot Sheep Whitefish Worsted: Moose Meadow (approx. 8-10 yd. / 7-9 m)
- **D:** *Aly Bee Workshop Merino Worsted: Pomegranate (approx. 4 yd. / 3 m)
- **E:** *Aly Bee Workshop Merino Worsted: Orchard (approx. 2 yd. / 1.75 m)

*Used in duplicate stitching

NEEDLES

- US size 5 / 3.75 mm, 16 in. / 40 cm circular knitting needles
- US size 8 / 5 mm, 16 in. / 40 cm circular knitting needles
- US size 8 / 5 mm, set of double-pointed needles (DPNs)
- (or size needed to obtain gauge)

Continued on next page

NOTIONS

3 stitch markers (two of one color and one of another color)

Cable needle (CN)

Tapestry needle for weaving in ends and working duplicate stitches

GAUGE

With larger needles, approx. 9½ stitches = 2 in. / 5 cm in stranded stockinette stitch, blocked.

Note: The many cable stitches in this design may cause your knitting to tighten up, resulting in a smaller hat. I moved up to a size 8 / 5 mm needle for this design (I normally use a 7 / 4.5 mm). If you already know you are a tight knitter (or just want a larger hat), you might want to go up to a size 9 / 5.5 mm, especially for Rows 1–23 of the charted pattern.

With smaller circular needles and color A, cast on 96 stitches. Place single color marker and join in the round, being careful not to twist stitches.

Work the following rib pattern for approximately 1½ to 2 in. / 4 to 5 cm:

Rib Pattern: *(K1, p2) 2 times, (k1, p1) 10 times, (k1, p2) 2 times. Repeat from * 2 more times. 32 stitches per repeat, 96 stitches total.

Switch to larger needles and work chart from right to left beginning on Row 1, bottom right corner. Chart repeats three times around the hat. Use remaining two stitch markers of another color to mark chart repeats.

Note: In order to avoid long "floats" (strands of yarn on the inside of the hat) and to help maintain your tension, do not carry a color more than three or four stitches without twisting the colors around each other in the back of work.

Tip: To avoid show-through of contrasting color yarn on the right side, be sure to catch floats behind a knit stitch rather than a purl. This gets tricky and takes a bit of concentration, as many of the knit stitches in columns 10–24 are part of a cable stitch.

Switch to DPNs when work becomes too small for circular needles.

FINISHING

After chart is complete, cut yarn leaving a 10 in. / 25.5 cm tail. Using a tapestry needle, weave tail through remaining stitches and pull tightly to close circle. Pull tail to inside and weave in all ends.

Block as desired. See page 13 for my favorite hat blocking technique.

After all blocking is complete, work duplicate stitches in colors and locations shown.

Optional: Using your favorite pom-pom making technique, make a 2-toned pom-pom and attach to top of hat.

KEY

■ **No Stitch**
The "no stitch" squares represent the stitches that were lost due to decreases earlier in the round. *Do not skip a stitch.* Simply treat these squares as if they do not exist.

□ **K**
Knit

⊡ **P**
Purl

S1
Slip one purlwise with yarn in back

K2tog
Knit 2 together

2/1 RC
Slip 1 stitch to cable needle and hold in back; k2; k1 from cable needle.

2/1 RPC
Slip 1 stitch to cable needle and hold in back; k2; p1 from cable needle.

2/1 LC
Slip 2 stitches to cable needle and hold in front; k1; k2 from cable needle.

2/1 LPC
Slip 2 stitches to cable needle and hold in front; p1; k2 from cable needle.

D **Dup**
Work duplicate stitches after all knitting and blocking is complete.

At the heart of this Midwest state lies a history rich in agriculture. With nearly 90 percent of its land used for farming, Iowa is the top producer of corn in the country, but also grows soybeans, red apples, and other crops. Rich soil and nearly level land combined with the right amount of rainfall and sunlight create the perfect conditions for the large farms and rows of crops that dominate the landscape. Aside from agriculture, Iowa is known as the birthplace of actor John Wayne, fictional character Captain James T. Kirk of *Star Trek*, and Otto Rohwedder, the man who invented the bread-slicing machine. One of the best inventions ever, right? Additionally, the famous Iowa State Fair attracts a million visitors from neighboring states (and around the world) every summer.

This design uses a fun and easy stitch pattern to depict diagonal rows of crops at sunrise. An optional farmhouse and silo are seen in the distance.

SIZE

One size fits an average adult size head (approx. 19 in. / 48 cm – 22 in. / 56 cm)

Finished Circumference: approx. 20¼ in. / 51.5 cm.

YARN

Worsted weight yarn (#4) in six colors. Shown in:

- **A:** Malabrigo Rios: Lettuce (40 g / 84 yd. / 77 m)
- **B:** Stunning String Studio Legacy Worsted: Black Forest (10 g / 21 yd. / 19 m)
- **C:** *Aly Bee Workshop Merino Worsted: Farmhouse (1-2 yd. / 1-1.75 m)
- **D:** Aly Bee Workshop Merino Worsted: Orchard (10 g / 20 yd. / 18 m)
- **E:** Aly Bee Workshop Merino Worsted: Smoothie (10 g / 20 yd. / 18m)
- **F:** Aly Bee Workshop Merino Worsted: Glass Slipper (15 g / 30 yd. / 27 m)

*Used only in duplicate stitching

Continued on next page

NEEDLES

- US size 5 / 3.75 mm, 16 in. / 40 cm circular knitting needles
- US size 7 / 4.5 mm, 16 in. / 40 cm circular knitting needles
- US size 7 / 4.5 mm, set of double-pointed needles (DPNs)
- (or size needed to obtain gauge)

NOTIONS

3 stitch markers (two of one color and one of another color)

Tapestry needle for weaving in ends and working duplicate stitches

GAUGE

With larger needles, approx. 9½ stitches = 2 in. / 5 cm in stranded stockinette stitch, blocked.

Note: If you already know you are a tight knitter (or just want a larger hat), go up one or two needle sizes for both the ribbing and the body of the hat.

With smaller circular needles and color A, cast on 96 stitches. Place single color marker and join in the round, being careful not to twist stitches.

Work (k2, p2) rib pattern for approximately 1½ to 2 in. / 4 to 5 cm.

Switch to larger needles and work chart from right to left beginning on Row 1, bottom right corner. Chart repeats three times around the hat. Use remaining two stitch markers of another color to mark chart repeats.

Note: In order to avoid long "floats" (strands of yarn on the inside of the hat) and to help maintain your tension, do not carry a color more than three or four stitches without twisting the colors around each other in the back of work.

Switch to DPNs when work becomes too small for circular needles.

FINISHING

After chart is complete, cut yarn leaving a 10 in. / 25.5 cm tail. Using a tapestry needle, weave tail through remaining stitches and pull tightly to close circle. Pull tail to inside and weave in all ends.

Block as desired. See page 13 for my favorite hat blocking technique.

Optional: After all blocking is complete, using duplicate stitches and color C (or another color of choice), add a farmhouse, barn, or silo where shown. See photo for inspiration. A cute house- or barn-shaped button could work too.

KEY

- ☐ K — Knit
- ⊡ P — Purl
- D Dup — Work duplicate stitches after all knitting and blocking is complete.
- V S1 — Slip one purlwise with yarn in back
- / K2tog — Knit 2 together
- ■ No Stitch — The "no stitch" squares represent the stitches that were lost due to decreases earlier in the round. *Do not skip a stitch.* Simply treat these squares as if they do not exist.

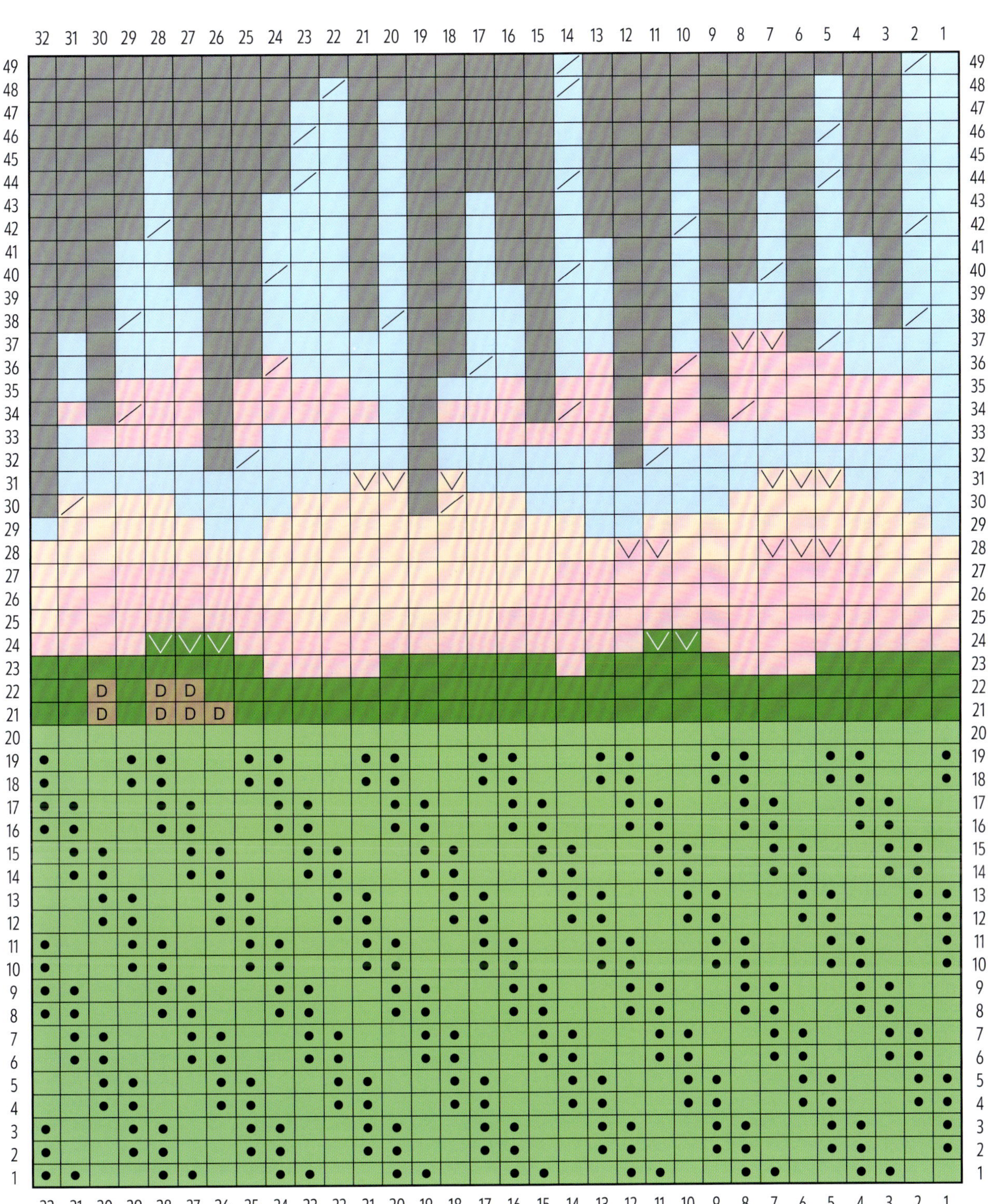

Nestled in the heart of the country, Kansas (nicknamed the Sunflower State) is known for farming, sprawling prairies and grasslands, cattle ranching, wind, gently rolling hills, and great barbecue, as well as a host of museums and historical sites like an underground salt museum! It's also the birthplace of Amelia Earhart and (of course) home to Dorothy from *The Wizard of Oz*.

But this design was inspired by one of the most famous features of Kansas—wheat fields! Just as the right soil and temperature combine to make Kansas one of the top wheat producers in the country, warm colors and a wheat-inspired stitch combine to create a design that captures the essence of wheat farming in Kansas. As John Denver once sang, "Gold is just a windy Kansas wheat field and blue is just a Kansas summer sky."

SIZE

One size fits an average adult size head. (Approx. 19 in. / 48 cm – 22 in. / 56 cm)

Finished Circumference: approx. 20¼ in. / 51.5 cm.

YARN

Worsted weight yarn (#4) in three colors. Shown in:

- **A:** Aly Bee Workshop Merino Worsted: Harvest (50 g / 100 yd. / 91 m)
- **B:** Stunning String Studio Legacy Worsted: Something Blue (20 g / 43 yd. / 39 m)
- **C:** Aly Bee Workshop Merino Worsted: Vanilla (13 g / 26 yd. / 24 m)

NEEDLES

- US size 5 / 3.75 mm, 16 in. / 40 cm circular knitting needles
- US size 7 / 4.5 mm, 16 in. / 40 cm circular knitting needles
- US size 7 / 4.5 mm, set of double-pointed needles (DPNs)
- (or size needed to obtain gauge)

Continued on next page

NOTIONS

3 stitch markers (two of one color and one of another color)

Tapestry needle for weaving in ends

Cable needle (CN)

GAUGE

With larger needles, approx. 9½ stitches = 2 in. / 5 cm in stranded stockinette stitch, blocked.

Note: If you already know you are a tight knitter (or just want a larger hat), go up one or two needle sizes for both the ribbing and the body of the hat.

With smaller circular needles and color A, cast on 96 stitches. Place single color marker and join in the round, being careful not to twist stitches.

Work rib pattern as follows for approximately 1½ to 2 in. / 4 to 5 cm:

Rib Pattern: *K1, p2, k1; repeat from * to end of round.

Switch to larger needles and work chart from right to left beginning on Row 1, bottom right corner. Chart repeats three times around the hat. Use remaining two stitch markers of another color to mark chart repeats.

Note: In order to avoid long "floats" (strands of yarn on the inside of the hat) and to help maintain your tension, do not carry a color more than three or four stitches without twisting the colors around each other in the back of work.

Switch to DPNs when work becomes too small for circular needles.

FINISHING

After chart is complete, cut yarn leaving a 10 in. / 25.5 cm tail. Using a tapestry needle, weave tail through remaining stitches and pull tightly to close circle. Pull tail to inside and weave in all ends.

Block as desired. See page 13 for my favorite hat blocking technique.

KEY

☐	K Knit
V	S1 Slip one purlwise with yarn in back. No need to carry this color across back of work in rows 31 and 32
1/2 RC	1/2 RC Slip 2 stitches to cable needle and hold in back; k1; k2 from cable needle.
1/2 LC	1/2 LC Slip 1 stitch to cable needle and hold in front; k2; k1 from cable needle.
1/1 RC	1/1 RC Slip 1 stitch to cable needle and hold in back; k1; k1 from cable needle.
1/1 LC	1/1 LC Slip 1 stitch to cable needle and hold in front; k1; k1 from cable needle
/	K2tog Knit 2 together
■	No Stitch The "no stitch" squares represent the stitches that were lost due to decreases earlier in the round. *Do not skip a stitch*. Simply treat these squares as if they do not exist.
\	ssk Slip, slip, knit: Slip 2 stitches knit-wise, place stitches back on left needle, knit 2 tog through back loop

Pictured Rocks National Lakeshore is one of the most visited and beautiful locations in Michigan. Miles and miles of sandstone cliffs towering fifty to two hundred feet above the shore of Lake Superior appear painted with a multitude of colors. As groundwater seeps through the cracks and crevices of the cliffs, it deposits streaks and layers of assorted colors, depending on the minerals in the water. Copper, iron, manganese, and limonite create blue, green, red, orange, brown, black, and white streaks. Nature's artwork! Continuous erosion from wind and water creates arches and caves that add to the beauty and uniqueness of the region. In the winter months, the scene changes to a snow-filled wonderland of winter activities ranging from snowshoeing to viewing ice formations, especially the beautiful ice curtains that look exactly as the name implies.

Above a beautiful blue Lake Superior, variegated yarns create colorful cliffs complete with sea caves and arches. The forests and blue sky invite exploration of the rest of the park.

SIZE

One size fits an average adult size head (approx. 19 in. / 48 cm – 22 in. / 56 cm)

Finished Circumference: approx. 20¼ in. / 51.5 cm.

YARN

Worsted weight yarn (#4) in seven colors. Shown in:

- **A:** Malabrigo Rios: Denim (25 g / 53 yd. / 48 m)
- **B:** Malabrigo Rios: Piedras (15 g / 32 yd. / 29 m)
- **C:** Aly Bee Workshop Merino Worsted: Spooky (10 g / 20 yd. / 18 m)
- **D:** Malabrigo Rios: Cielo Y Tierra (10 g / 21 yd. / 19 m)
- **E:** Malabrigo Rios: Camel (5 g / 10 yd. / 9 m)
- **F:** Stunning String Studio Legacy Worsted: Pine Bough (15 g / 32 yd. / 29 m)
- **G:** Malabrigo Rios: Aquamarine (20 g / 42 yd. / 38 m)

Continued on next page

NEEDLES

- US size 5 / 3.75 mm, 16 in. / 40 cm circular knitting needles
- US size 7 / 4.5 mm, 16 in. / 40 cm circular knitting needles
- US size 7 / 4.5 mm, set of double-pointed needles (DPNs)
- (or size needed to obtain gauge)

NOTIONS

3 stitch markers (two of one color and one of another color)

Tapestry needle for weaving in ends and working duplicate stitches

GAUGE

With larger needles, approx. 9½ stitches = 2 in. / 5 cm in stranded stockinette stitch, blocked.

Note: If you already know you are a tight knitter (or just want a larger hat), go up one or two needle sizes for both the ribbing and the body of the hat.

With smaller circular needles and color A, cast on 96 stitches. Place single color marker and join in the round, being careful not to twist stitches.

Work (k1, p1) rib pattern for approximately 1½ to 2 in. / 4 to 5 cm.

Switch to larger needles and work chart from right to left beginning on Row 1, bottom right corner. Chart repeats three times around the hat. Use remaining two stitch markers of another color to mark chart repeats.

Note: In order to avoid long "floats" (strands of yarn on the inside of the hat) and to help maintain your tension, do not carry a color more than three or four stitches without twisting the colors around each other in the back of work.

Switch to DPNs when work becomes too small for circular needles.

FINISHING

After chart is complete, cut yarn leaving a 10 in. / 25.5 tail. Using a tapestry needle, weave tail through remaining stitches and pull tightly to close circle. Pull tail to inside and weave in all ends.

Block as desired. See page 13 for my favorite hat blocking technique.

After all knitting and blocking is complete, work duplicate stitches where shown using color A.

KEY

- ☐ K — Knit
- D Dup — Work duplicate stitches after all knitting and blocking is complete.
- V S1 — Slip one purlwise with yarn in back
- / K2tog — Knit 2 together
- ■ No Stitch — The "no stitch" squares represent the stitches that were lost due to decreases earlier in the round. *Do not skip a stitch.* Simply treat these squares as if they do not exist.

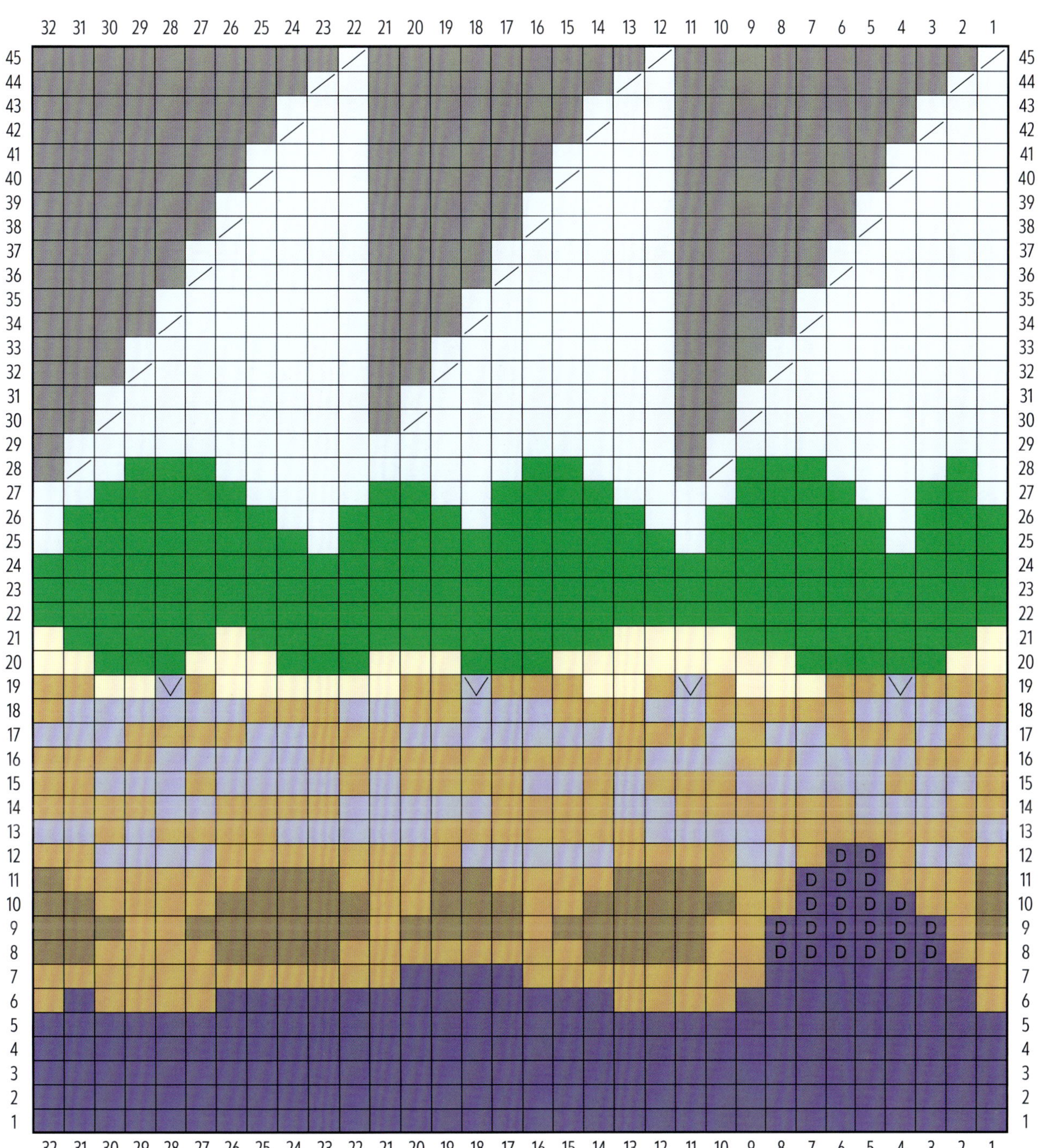

Commonly referred to as the Land of 10,000 Lakes, Minnesota embraces every type of water activity imaginable from boating and kayaking to paddleboarding and year-round fishing or simply gazing out at the water from a cozy cabin. Minnesota is ranked as a top location in the country for ice fishing, even hosting the world's largest ice fishing competition every January. Vacationing by houseboat is also a wonderful way to explore the lakes, especially in Voyageurs National Park, where you can stop at a remote island for the night and gaze at the stars while listening to the mournful calls of loons. Minnesota also boasts beautiful forests chock-full of wildlife, rivers, and waterfalls, as well as amazing hiking and camping with spectacular views. If city life is more your style, big cities and smaller towns alike offer all sorts of museums, galleries, concert venues, and restaurants featuring local and international cuisine.

Lakes, loons, and lily pads feature prominently in this easy-to-knit design. A touch of simple embroidery adds detail to the loons and lily pads.

SIZE

One size fits an average adult size head (approx. 19 in. / 48 cm – 22 in. / 56 cm)

Finished Circumference: approx. 20¼ in. / 51.5 cm.

YARN

Worsted weight yarn (#4) in five colors. Shown in:

- **A:** Aly Bee Workshop Merino Worsted: Count Chocula (25 g / 50 yd. / 46 m)
- **B:** Peekaboo Yarns Merino Worsted: Zion Blue (33 g / 71 yd. / 65 m)
- **C:** Aly Bee Workshop Merino Worsted: Fresh Cut (20 g / 40 yd. / 37 m)
- **D:** Malabrigo Rios: Black (10 g / 21 yd. / 19 m)
- **E:** Aly Bee Workshop Merino Worsted: Vanilla (5 g / 10 yd. / 9 m)

Approx. 3 yd. / 2.75 m of any red yarn to make French knot eyes on the loons.

Continued on next page

NEEDLES

- US size 4 / 3.5 mm, 16 in. / 40 cm circular knitting needles
- US size 7 / 4.5 mm, 16 in. / 40 cm circular knitting needles
- US size 7 / 4.5 mm, set of double-pointed needles (DPNs)
- (or size needed to obtain gauge)

NOTIONS

3 stitch markers (two of one color and one of another color)

Tapestry needle for weaving in ends and working duplicate stitches and embroidery

GAUGE

With larger needles, approx. 9½ stitches = 2 in. / 5 cm in stranded stockinette stitch, blocked.

Note: If you already know you are a tight knitter (or just want a larger hat) go up one or two needle sizes for both the ribbing and the body of the hat.

With smaller circular needles and color A, cast on 96 stitches. Place single color marker and join in the round, being careful not to twist stitches.

Work the following rib pattern:

***Note:** This rib pattern is not as compact as other rib patterns, so I used a size 4 / 3.5 mm needle to be sure it was snug enough.

Round 1: *K2, p1; repeat from * to end of round.

Round 2: *K1, p2; repeat from * to end of round.

Repeat Rounds 1 and 2 until ribbing measures 1½ to 2 in. / 4 to 5 cm, ending with Round 2.

Switch to larger needles and work chart from right to left beginning on Row 1, bottom right corner. Chart repeats 3 times around the hat. Use remaining two stitch markers of another color to mark chart repeats.

Note: In order to avoid long "floats" (strands of yarn on the inside of the hat) and to help maintain your tension, do not carry a color more than three or four stitches without twisting the colors around each other in the back of work.

Switch to DPNs when work becomes too small for circular needles.

FINISHING

After chart is complete, cut yarn leaving a 10 in. / 25.5 cm tail. Using a tapestry needle, weave tail through remaining stitches and pull tightly to close circle. Pull tail to inside and weave in all ends.

Block as desired. See page 13 for my favorite hat blocking technique.

After all blocking is complete, work duplicate stitches where shown in color E. Add half duplicate stitches or small straight stitches as desired to complete the additional markings on the loons in color E. This does not have to be precise. Also in color E (or any other desired color), use straight stitches to add blooms to all or some of the lily pads. Using color D, extend the beaks using straight stitches. Add red French knots for the eyes. See photo for inspiration.

KEY

☐ **K**
Knit

D **Dup**
Work duplicate stitches after all knitting and blocking is complete.

⧄ **K2tog**
Knit 2 together

■ **No Stitch**
The "no stitch" squares represent the stitches that were lost due to decreases earlier in the round. *Do not skip a stitch*. Simply treat these squares as if they do not exist.

⧅ **SSK**
Slip, slip, knit: Slip 2 stitches purlwise. Place stitches back on left needle and knit through both stitches through back loop.

If you love caves, you'll love Missouri! With approximately seven thousand documented caves of all sizes and shapes, Missouri is often called the Cave State. Nature's perfect combination of rainfall, underground aquafers, and soluble rock over millions of years has created caves with beautiful formations, waterfalls, rivers, and seemingly endless passageways. Man's ingenuity has created exciting ways to explore many of them. In the caves of Missouri, you can ride a boat or a golf cart past waterfalls, scuba dive to antique mining equipment, or simply take a stroll by lantern light as early explorers did. You'll even find caves that served as literary inspiration for Mark Twain and (according to local legend) a hideout for outlaw Jesse James.

In this artistic and stylized interpretation of waterfalls and caves, three shades of blue represent water seeping through cracks in the gray bedrock. An abstract yet classic design.

SIZE

One size fits an average adult size head (approx. 19 in. / 48 cm – 22 in. / 56 cm)

Finished Circumference: approx. 20¼ in. / 51.5 cm.

YARN

Worsted weight yarn (#4) in four colors. Shown in:

- **A:** Malabrigo Rios: Bobby Blue (33 g / 69 yd. / 63 m)
- **B:** Stunning String Studio Legacy Worsted: Charcoal (20 g / 43 yd. / 39 m)
- **C:** Malabrigo Rios: Cosmos (20 g / 42 yd. / 38 m)
- **D:** Peekaboo Yarns Merino Worsted: Zion Blue (15 g / 32 yd. / 29 m)

NEEDLES

- US size 5 / 3.75 mm, 16 in. / 40 cm circular knitting needles
- US size 7 / 4.5 mm, 16 in. / 40 cm circular knitting needles
- US size 7 / 4.5 mm, set of double-pointed needles (DPNs)
- (or size needed to obtain gauge)

Continued on next page

NOTIONS

3 stitch markers (two of one color and one of another color)

Tapestry needle for weaving in ends

GAUGE

With larger needles, approx. 9½ stitches = 2 in. / 5 cm in stranded stockinette stitch, blocked.

Note: If you already know you are a tight knitter (or just want a larger hat), go up one or two needle sizes for both the ribbing and the body of the hat.

With smaller circular needles and color A, cast on 96 stitches. Place single color marker and join in the round, being careful not to twist stitches.

Work (k1 tbl, p1) rib pattern for approximately 1½ to 2 in. / 4 to 5 cm.
(tbl=through back loop)

Switch to larger needles and work chart from right to left beginning on Row 1, bottom right corner. Chart repeats three times around the hat. Use remaining two stitch markers of another color to mark chart repeats.

Note: In order to avoid long "floats" (strands of yarn on the inside of the hat) and to help maintain your tension, do not carry a color more than three or four stitches without twisting the colors around each other in the back of work.

Switch to DPNs when work becomes too small for circular needles.

FINISHING

After chart is complete, cut yarn leaving a 10 in. / 25.5 cm tail. Using a tapestry needle, weave tail through remaining stitches and pull tightly to close circle. Pull tail to inside and weave in all ends.

Block as desired. See page 13 for my favorite hat blocking technique.

KEY

☐ K
Knit

☑ S1
Slip one purlwise with yarn in back

⧄ K2tog
Knit 2 together

■ No Stitch
The "no stitch" squares represent the stitches that were lost due to decreases earlier in the round. *Do not skip a stitch*. Simply treat these squares as if they do not exist.

Covering nearly one-third of the state, the undulating landscape of the Sandhills region of Nebraska contains naturally formed pockets of lakes, rivers, marshes, and wetlands. These ancient sand dunes (now stabilized with grasses) have served as stopover grounds for migratory birds for thousands of years, including the famous sandhill cranes. This early spring migration brings five hundred thousand to one million cranes to this otherwise quiet region every year, attracting bird-watchers, scientists, and photographers from around the world.

This design captures the beloved cranes in flight over the grasslands on a sunny morning. Use duplicate stitching to add a few birds resting in the grass.

SIZE

One size fits an average adult size head (approx. 19 in. / 48 cm – 22 in. / 56 cm)

Finished Circumference: approx. 20¼ in. / 51.5 cm.

YARN

Worsted weight yarn (#4) in five colors. Shown in:

- **A:** Aly Bee Workshop Merino Worsted: Harvest (25 g / 50 yd. / 46 m)
- **B:** Malabrigo Rios: Sandstorm (15 g /32 yd. / 29 m)
- **C:** Polka Dot Sheep Whitefish Worsted: Moose Meadow (5 g / 11 yd. / 10 m)
- **D:** Stunning String Studio Legacy Worsted: Cornflower Blue (33 g / 71 yd. / 65 m)
- **E:** Malabrigo Rios: Natural (15 g / 32 yd. / 29m)

Continued on next page

NEEDLES

- US size 5 / 3.75 mm, 16 in. / 40 cm circular knitting needles
- US size 7 / 4.5 mm, 16 in. / 40 cm circular knitting needles
- US size 7 / 4.5 mm, set of double-pointed needles (DPNs)
- (or size needed to obtain gauge)

NOTIONS

3 stitch markers (two of one color and one of another color)

Tapestry needle for weaving in ends and working duplicate stitches

GAUGE

With larger needles, approx. 9½ stitches = 2 in. / 5 cm in stranded stockinette stitch, blocked.

Note: If you already know you are a tight knitter (or just want a larger hat), go up one or two needle sizes for both the ribbing and the body of the hat.

With smaller circular needles and color A, cast on 96 stitches. Place single color marker and join in the round, being careful not to twist stitches.

Work (k1, p1) rib pattern for approximately 1½ to 2 in. / 4 to 5 cm.

Switch to larger needles and work chart from right to left beginning on Row 1, bottom right corner. Chart repeats three times around the hat. Use remaining two stitch markers of another color to mark chart repeats.

Note: In order to avoid long "floats" (strands of yarn on the inside of the hat) and to help maintain your tension, do not carry a color more than three or four stitches without twisting the colors around each other in the back of work.

Switch to DPNs when work becomes too small for circular needles.

FINISHING

After chart is complete, cut yarn leaving a 10 in. / 25.5 cm tail. Using a tapestry needle, weave tail through remaining stitches and pull tightly to close circle. Pull tail to inside and weave in all ends.

Block as desired. See page 13 for my favorite hat blocking technique.

Optional: After all blocking is complete, to add a few cranes that have landed in the field, work duplicate stitches where shown using color B and a tapestry needle.

KEY

☐ K
Knit

D Dup
Work duplicate stitches after all knitting and blocking is complete.

V S1
Slip one purlwise with yarn in back

/ K2tog
Knit 2 together

■ No Stitch
The "no stitch" squares represent the stitches that were lost due to decreases earlier in the round. *Do not skip a stitch.* Simply treat these squares as if they do not exist.

North Dakota has very few trees. As part of the Great Plains region, the climate and topograhy of the state favor grasslands and prairies over forests. Throughout the years, especially in the 1930s, farmers and homeowners have planted rows of trees as protection against the harsh winters and damaging winds. Many of these windbreaks are still standing today with some impressively tall trees. But most of the largest and tallest in the state can be found in the city of Fargo, where trees have been planted for decades as urban forests. The trees beautify the city, provide shade and shelter, and improve the environment.

This design features a tree-lined street in Fargo on a very snowy winter day. As the snow blankets the neighborhood, the colors of houses and cars are nearly imperceptible, creating a beautiful almost sepia-toned scene.

SIZE

One size fits an average adult size head (approx. 19 in. / 48 cm – 22 in. / 56 cm)

Finished Circumference: approx. 20¼ in. / 51.5 cm.

YARN

Worsted weight yarn (#4) in three colors. Shown in:

- **A:** Malabrigo Rios: Natural (75 g / 158 yd. / 144 m)
- **B:** Stunning String Studio Legacy Worsted: Dark Camel (25 g / 54 yd. / 49 m)
- **C:** *Polka Dot Sheep Whitefish Worsted: Scapegoat (10 g / 21 yd. / 19 m)

*Used only in duplicate stitching

NEEDLES

- US size 5 / 3.75 mm, 16 in. / 40 cm circular knitting needles
- US size 7 / 4.5 mm, 16 in. / 40 cm circular knitting needles
- US size 7 / 4.5 mm, set of double-pointed needles (DPNs)
- (or size needed to obtain gauge)

Continued on next page

NOTIONS

3 stitch markers (two of one color and one of another color)

Tapestry needle for weaving in ends and working duplicate stitches

GAUGE

With larger needles, approx. 9½ stitches = 2 in. / 5 cm in stranded stockinette stitch, blocked.

Note: If you already know you are a tight knitter (or just want a larger hat), go up one or two needle sizes for both the ribbing and the body of the hat.

With smaller circular needles and color A, cast on 96 stitches. Place single color marker and join in the round being careful to not twist stitches.

Work (k2, p2) rib pattern for approximately 4 in. / 10 cm for a fold-over ribbing/brim as shown, or 1½ to 2 in. / 4 to 5 cm for a single layer ribbing/brim.

Switch to larger needles and work chart from right to left beginning on Row 1, bottom right corner. Chart repeats three times around the hat. Use remaining two stitch markers of another color to mark chart repeats.

Note: If you are comfortable knitting with 3 colors in a row, simply ignore the "D" symbols and knit the color C stitches where shown.

Note: In order to avoid long "floats" (strands of yarn on the inside of the hat) and to help maintain your tension, do not carry a color more than three or four stitches without twisting the colors around each other in the back of work.

Switch to DPNs when work becomes too small for circular needles.

FINISHING

After chart is complete, cut yarn leaving a 10 in. / 25.5 cm tail. Using a tapestry needle, weave tail through remaining stitches and pull tightly to close circle. Pull tail to inside and weave in all ends.

Block as desired. See page 13 for my favorite hat blocking technique.

After all knitting and blocking is complete, work duplicate stitches in color C where shown. If you prefer trees without the "neighborhood," simply omit the duplicate stitching.

KEY

☐ **K** Knit

[D] **Dup** Work duplicate stitches after all knitting and blocking is complete.

● **Mb** Mini bobble: (p1, k1, p1, k1) into next stitch, then lift 2nd, 3rd, and 4th stitches over first stitch and off needle, one at a time.

⁄ **K2tog** Knit 2 together

■ **No Stitch** The "no stitch" squares represent the stitches that were lost due to decreases earlier in the round. *Do not skip a stitch.* Simply treat these squares as if they do not exist.

V **S1** Slip one purlwise with yarn in back

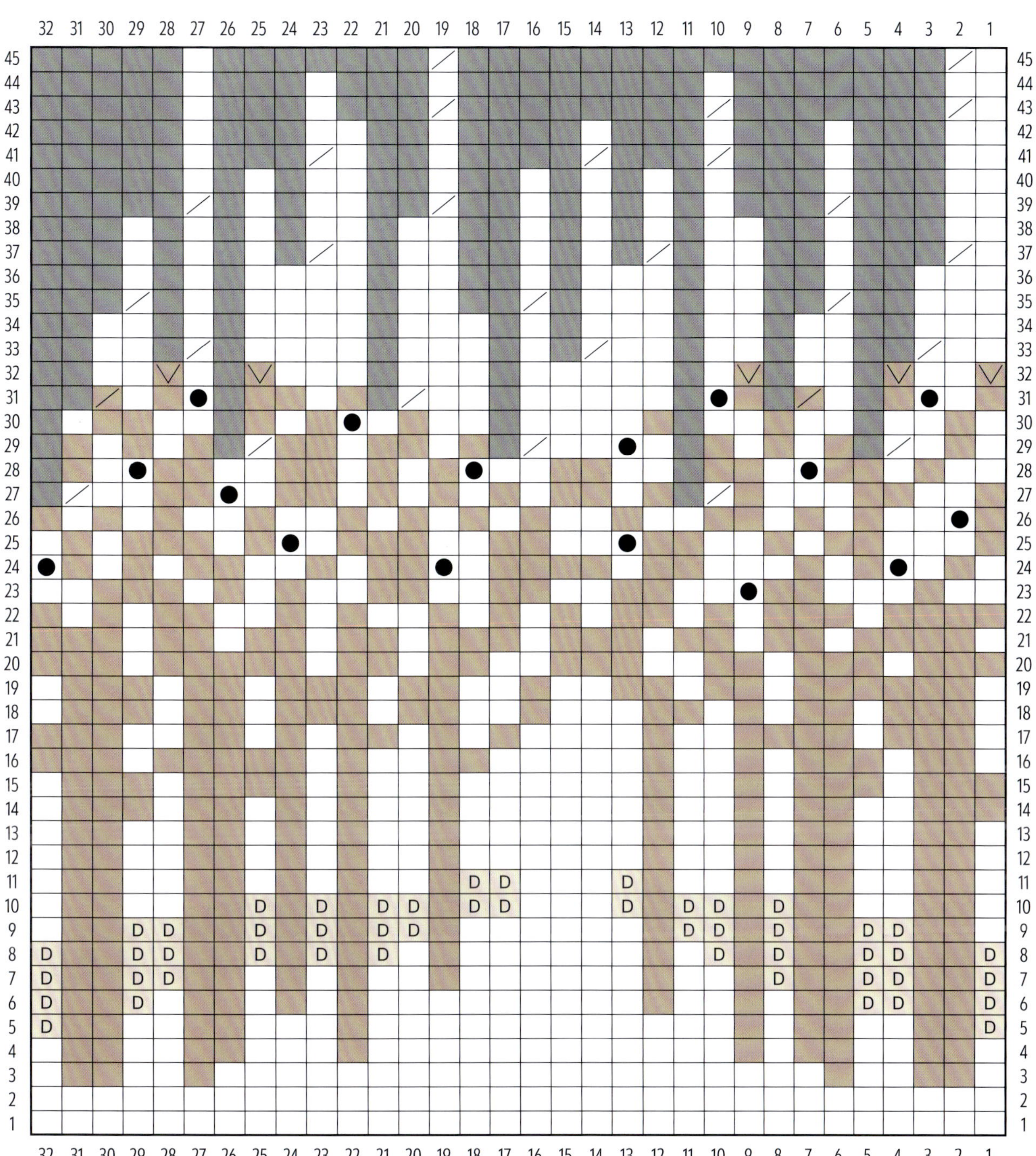

Buckeye trees and buckeye nuts have become synonymous with Ohio and the people who live there. So much so, it seems nearly impossible to mention Ohio without mentioning buckeyes. The tree gets its name from the nut it produces, which resembles the color and shape of a deer's eye. The Ohio buckeye is the official state tree, the state nickname (the Buckeye State), and the official mascot of The Ohio State University. The nuts (although inedible) are thought to bring good luck if you carry one in your pocket. There's even a popular buckeye candy, a peanut-butter ball dipped in chocolate with a circle of peanut butter left exposed to resemble the nut. Sounds delicious to me! The residents of Ohio are also referred to as Buckeyes. No other state has embraced a symbol with such zeal as Ohioans have with their buckeye trees.

This designs embraces the beloved state tree with a band of easily recognizable buckeye nuts topped with a row of buckeye trees under a clear blue sky.

SIZE

One size fits an average adult size head (approx. 19 in. / 48 cm – 22 in. / 56 cm)

Finished Circumference: approx. 20¼ in. / 51.5 cm.

YARN

Worsted weight yarn (#4) in four colors. Shown in:

A: Malabrigo Rios: Ivy (40 g / 84 yd. / 77 m)

B: Stunning String Studio Legacy Worsted: Desert Floor (15 g / 32 yd. / 29 m)

C: Aly Bee Workshop Merino Worsted: Semisweet (15 g / 30 yd. / 27 m)

D: Polka Dot Sheep Whitefish Worsted: Storm Chaser (33 g / 72 yd. / 66 m)

NEEDLES

- US size 5 / 3.75 mm, 16 in. / 40 cm circular knitting needles
- US size 7 / 4.5 mm, 16 in. / 40 cm circular knitting needles
- US size 7 / 4.5 mm, set of double-pointed needles (DPNs)
- (or size needed to obtain gauge)

Continued on next page

NOTIONS

3 stitch markers (two of one color and one of another color)

Tapestry needle for weaving in ends and working duplicate stitches

GAUGE

With larger needles, approx. 9½ stitches = 2 in. / 5 cm in stranded stockinette stitch, blocked.

Note: If you already know you are a tight knitter (or just want a larger hat), go up one or two needle sizes for both the ribbing and the body of the hat.

With smaller circular needles and color A, cast on 96 stitches. Place single color marker and join in the round, being careful not to twist stitches.

Work (k1, p1) rib pattern for approximately 1½ to 2 in. / 4 to 5 cm.

Switch to larger needles and work chart from right to left beginning on Row 1, bottom right corner. Chart repeats three times around the hat. Use remaining two stitch markers of another color to mark chart repeats.

Note: In order to avoid long "floats" (strands of yarn on the inside of the hat) and to help maintain your tension, do not carry a color more than three or four stitches without twisting the colors around each other in the back of work.

Switch to DPNs when work becomes too small for circular needles.

FINISHING

After chart is complete, cut yarn leaving a 10 in. / 25.5 cm tail. Using a tapestry needle, weave tail through remaining stitches and pull tightly to close circle. Pull tail to inside and weave in all ends.

Block as desired. See page 13 for my favorite hat blocking technique.

KEY

- ☐ K — Knit
- ☑ S1 — Slip one purlwise with yarn in back
- ◫ K2tog — Knit 2 together
- ■ No Stitch — The "no stitch" squares represent the stitches that were lost due to decreases earlier in the round. *Do not skip a stitch*. Simply treat these squares as if they do not exist.

Driving through South Dakota can feel like driving through several different states not only because of its sheer size, but also because of the vast geographical differences between the various regions. You could be sailing on a lake one day and then hiking through colorful badlands or exploring caves on another. One day might include a drive through vast national grasslands with huge bison herds (and some of the biggest skies you've ever seen), while another finds you picnicking in forests or near waterfalls. You might even end up on the stunning Needles Highway, a fourteen-mile scenic drive in the Black Hills that takes you through forests, meadows, and spectacular otherworldly granite formations. The twists and turns of the road reveal something new around every corner. Wherever you go in South Dakota, the scenery ranges from breathtaking to serene, while the connection to Native American culture is palpable.

This fun, knitted interpretation of the Needles Highway features plenty of granite spires and a few button-shaped cars on the winding road.

SIZE

One size fits an average adult size head (approx. 19 in. / 48 cm – 22 in. / 56 cm)

Finished Circumference: approx. 20¼ in. / 51.5 cm.

YARN

Worsted weight yarn (#4) in five colors. Shown in:

- **A:** Stunning String Studio Legacy Worsted: Black Forest (20 g / 43 yd. / 39 m)
- **B:** Polka Dot Sheep Whitefish Worsted: Barnwood (20 g / 43 yd. / 39 m)
- **C:** Peekaboo Yarns Merino Worsted: Classic Silver (10 g / 21 yd. / 19 m)
- **D:** Aly Bee Workshop Merino Worsted: Glass Slipper (33 g / 66 yd. / 60 m)
- **E:** Malabrigo Rios: Natural (10 g / 21 yd. / 19 m)

Continued on next page

NEEDLES

- US size 5 / 3.75 mm, 16 in. / 40 cm circular knitting needles
- US size 7 / 4.5 mm, 16 in. / 40 cm circular knitting needles
- US size 7 / 4.5 mm, set of double-pointed needles (DPNs)
  (or size needed to obtain gauge)

NOTIONS

3 stitch markers (two of one color and one of another color)

Tapestry needle for weaving in ends and working duplicate stitches

Optional: car shaped buttons and any thread and needle to attach them.

GAUGE

With larger needles, approx. 9½ stitches = 2 in. / 5 cm in stranded stockinette stitch, blocked.

Note: If you already know you are a tight knitter (or just want a larger hat), go up one or two needle sizes for both the ribbing and the body of the hat.

With smaller circular needles and color A, cast on 96 stitches. Place single color marker and join in the round, being careful not to twist stitches.

Work (k2, p2) rib pattern for approximately 1½ to 2 in. / 4 to 5 cm.

Switch to larger needles and work chart from right to left beginning on Row 1, bottom right corner. Chart repeats three times around the hat. Use remaining two stitch markers of another color to mark chart repeats.

Note: In order to avoid long "floats" (strands of yarn on the inside of the hat) and to help maintain your tension, do not carry a color more than three or four stitches without twisting the colors around each other in the back of work.

Switch to DPNs when work becomes too small for circular needles.

FINISHING

After chart is complete, cut yarn leaving a 10 in. / 25.5 cm tail. Using a tapestry needle, weave tail through remaining stitches and pull tightly to close circle. Pull tail to inside and weave in all ends.

Block as desired. See page 13 for my favorite hat blocking technique.

After all blocking is complete, work duplicate stitches where shown using color A.

Optional: Sew car shaped buttons along the road.

KEY

☐	K	Knit
●	P	Purl
V	S1	Slip one purlwise with yarn in back
D	Dup	Work duplicate stitches after all knitting and blocking is complete.
/	K2tog	Knit 2 together
■	No Stitch	The "no stitch" squares represent the stitches that were lost due to decreases earlier in the round. *Do not skip a stitch*. Simply treat these squares as if they do not exist.

Wisconsin has a long history in the lumber and beer industries. With nearly half of the state covered in forests, lumber has been an important part of the economy since the 1890s. And the beer? From legendary labels to homegrown craft breweries, Milwaukee in particular is world-renowned for producing amazing beer. But it's the dairy industry that reigns supreme in Wisconsin. Whether it's butter, cheese, ice cream, or milk, Wisconsin-made dairy products have been earning blue ribbons, gold medals, and distinguished awards year after year for decades. Think of the most buttery Swiss cheese ever or cheddar that has aged for more than fifteen years! Yum! Truly a cheese lover's paradise! Even the residents of Wisconsin proudly embrace their dairy heritage by wearing cheese-shaped hats at sports events and beyond.

Celebrate dairy products with a green pasture, a cow-print band, and a fun cheese-inspired pattern, topped off with simple knit stitches in the color of milk.

SIZE

One size fits an average adult size head (approx. 19 in. / 48 cm – 22 in. / 56 cm)

Finished Circumference: approx. 20¼ in. / 51.5 cm.

YARN

Worsted weight yarn (#4) in four colors. Shown in:

A: Aly Bee Workshop Merino Worsted: Fresh Cut (not shown on charts) (20 g / 40 yd. / 37 m)

B: Stunning String Studio Legacy Worsted: Shadow (20 g / 43 yd. / 39 m)

C: Aly Bee Workshop Merino Worsted: Sweet Cream (20 g / 40 yd. / 37 m)

D: Aly Bee Workshop Merino Worsted: Cheddar (40 g / 80 yd. / 73 m)

NEEDLES

- US size 5 / 3.75 mm, 16 in. / 40 cm circular knitting needles
- US size 7 / 4.5 mm, 16 in. / 40 cm circular knitting needles
- US size 7 / 4.5 mm, set of double-pointed needles (DPNs)
- (or size needed to obtain gauge)

Continued on next page

NOTIONS

3 stitch markers (two of one color and one of another color)

Cable needle (CN)

Tapestry needle for weaving in ends

GAUGE

With larger needles, approx. 9½ stitches = 2 in. / 5 cm in stranded stockinette stitch, blocked.

Note: If you already know you are a tight knitter (or just want a larger hat), go up one or two needle sizes for both the ribbing and the body of the hat.

With smaller circular needles and color A, cast on 96 stitches. Place single color marker and join in the round, being careful not to twist stitches.

Work (k1, p1) rib pattern for approximately 1½ to 2 in. / 4 to 5 cm.

Switch to larger needles and work **Wisconsin Chart #1** from right to left, beginning on Row 1, bottom right corner. Chart repeats three times around the hat. Use remaining two stitch markers of another color to mark chart repeats.

Note: In order to avoid long "floats" (strands of yarn on the inside of the hat) and to help maintain your tension, do not carry a color more than three or four stitches without twisting the colors around each other in the back of work.

Increase Round: After Wisconsin Chart #1 is complete, work increase round as follows: *K12, m1L (make one left); repeat from * to end of round - 104 stitches total.

After increase round is complete, work **Wisconsin Chart #2** from right to left, beginning on Row 1, bottom right corner. Chart repeats 13 times around the hat. Using stitch markers to mark chart repeats is optional but not necessary at this point. The chart is easy to keep track of without them. Be sure to continue to use a stitch marker at the beginning of round.

Switch to DPNs when work becomes too small for circular needles.

FINISHING

After chart is complete, cut yarn leaving a 10 in. / 25.5 cm tail. Using a tapestry needle, weave tail through remaining stitches and pull tightly to close circle. Pull tail to inside and weave in all ends.

Block as desired. See page 13 for my favorite hat blocking technique.

Chart 1

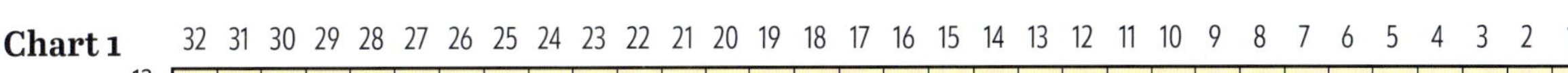

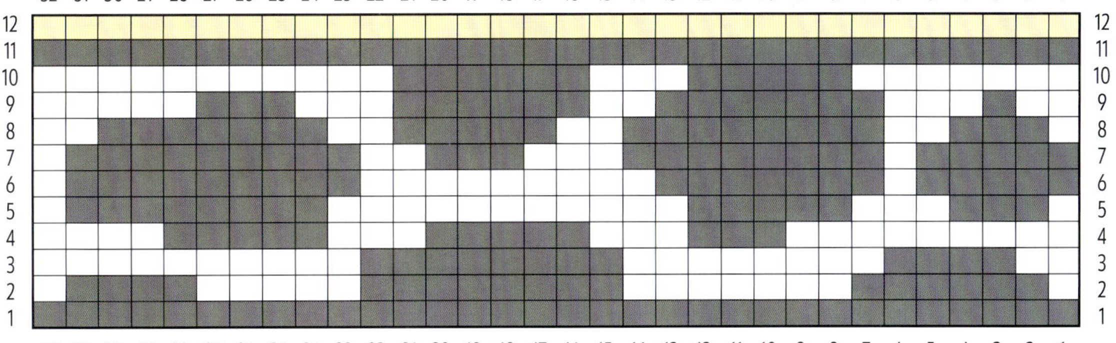

Chart 2

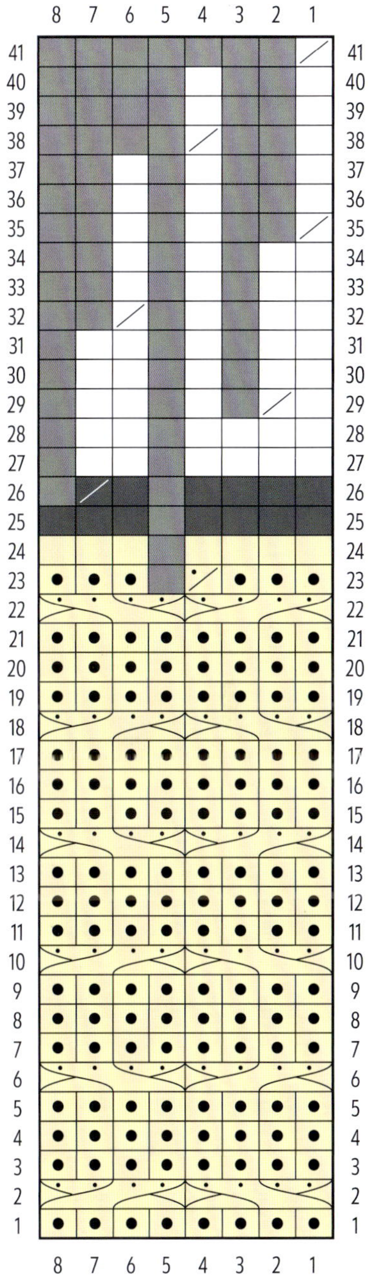

KEY

P
Purl

2/2 LPC
2/2 left Purl Cable: Slip 2 stitches to cable needle and hold in front; p2; p2 from cable needle.

2/2 RPC
2/2 Right Purl Cable: Slip 2 stitches to cable needle and hold in back; p2; p2 from cable needle.

P2tog
Purl 2 together

No Stitch
The "no stitch" squares represent the stitches that were lost due to decreases earlier in the round. *Do not skip a stitch*. Simply treat these squares as if they do not exist.

K
Knit

K2tog
Knit 2 together

THE WEST

Alaska

Arizona

California

Colorado

Hawaii

Idaho

Montana

Nevada

New Mexico

Oklahoma

Oregon

Texas

Utah

Washington

Wyoming

It's no surprise that Alaska is one of the snowiest of all fifty states. With one-third of the state above the Arctic Circle, dozens of mountain peaks over ten thousand feet, and winters with very little sunlight, you're going to have a lot of snow! In much of the state, snow stays on the ground for six months or more, and in the highest peaks, it never leaves. It's no wonder skiing, dogsledding, and snowmobiling are common winter activities for residents and visitors alike. Living with so much snow has its challenges, but it sure is beautiful! Whether it's blanketing the landscape, turning trees into frozen sculptures, or gently floating to the ground, there's nothing quite like the beauty and artistry of an individual snowflake that makes it all seem magical!

A hint of sparkle, stylized snowflakes, and a fun-to-knit texture that resembles tiny snowflakes create a design that captures the chill and beauty of snow in a warm and cozy hat. A fold-over ribbing adds extra warmth.

SIZE

One size fits an average adult size head (approx. 19 in. / 48 cm – 22 in. / 56 cm)

Finished Circumference: approx. 20¼ in. / 51.5 cm.

YARN

Worsted weight* yarn (#4) in two colors. Shown in:

- ☐ **A:** Stunning String Studio Twinkle DK*: Natural (75 g / 173 yd. / 158 m)
- ☐ **B:** Malabrigo Rios: Cosmos (33 g / 69 yd. / 63 m)

*Important: Although this yarn is DK weight, it worked up like a worsted weight for me. I chose it for the sparkle. If you use a different brand of DK, be sure to check your gauge as it may not work up the same. You can also use a natural or white worsted weight yarn without the sparkle.

Note: The amount of color A listed does include enough for a large pom-pom.

Continued on next page

NEEDLES

- US size 5 / 3.75 mm, 16 in. / 40 cm circular knitting needles
- US size 7 / 4.5 mm, 16 in. / 40 cm circular knitting needles
- US size 7 / 4.5 mm, set of double-pointed needles (DPNs)
- (or size needed to obtain gauge)

NOTIONS

3 stitch markers (two of one color and one of another color)

Tapestry needle for weaving in ends.

GAUGE

With larger needles, approx. 9½ stitches = 2 in. / 5 cm in stranded stockinette stitch, blocked.

Note: If you already know you are a tight knitter (or just want a larger hat), go up one or two needle sizes for both the ribbing and the body of the hat.

With smaller circular needles and color A, cast on 96 stitches. Place marker and join in the round, being careful not to twist stitches.

Work in (k1, p1) rib pattern for approximately 4 in. / 10 cm for a fold-over ribbing/brim as shown or approximately 1½ to 2 in. / 4 to 5 cm. for a single layer ribbing.

Switch to larger needles and work chart from right to left beginning on Row 1, bottom right corner. Chart repeats three times around the hat. Use remaining two stitch markers of another color to mark chart repeats.

Note: In order to avoid long "floats" (strands of yarn on the inside of the hat) and to help maintain your tension, do not carry a color more than three or four stitches without twisting the colors around each other in the back of work.

Switch to DPNs when work becomes too small for circular needles.

FINISHING

After chart is complete, cut yarn leaving a 10 in. / 25.5 cm tail. Using a tapestry needle, weave tail through remaining stitches and pull tightly to close circle. Pull tail to inside and weave in all ends.

Block as desired. See page 13 for my favorite hat blocking technique.

Optional: Using your favorite method, make a pom-pom using color A and attach to top of hat.

KEY

- ☐ K — Knit
- ⊡ P — Purl
- ⧄ K2tog — Knit 2 together
- ■ No Stitch — The "no stitch" squares represent the stitches that were lost due to decreases earlier in the round. *Do not skip a stitch.* Simply treat these squares as if they do not exist.

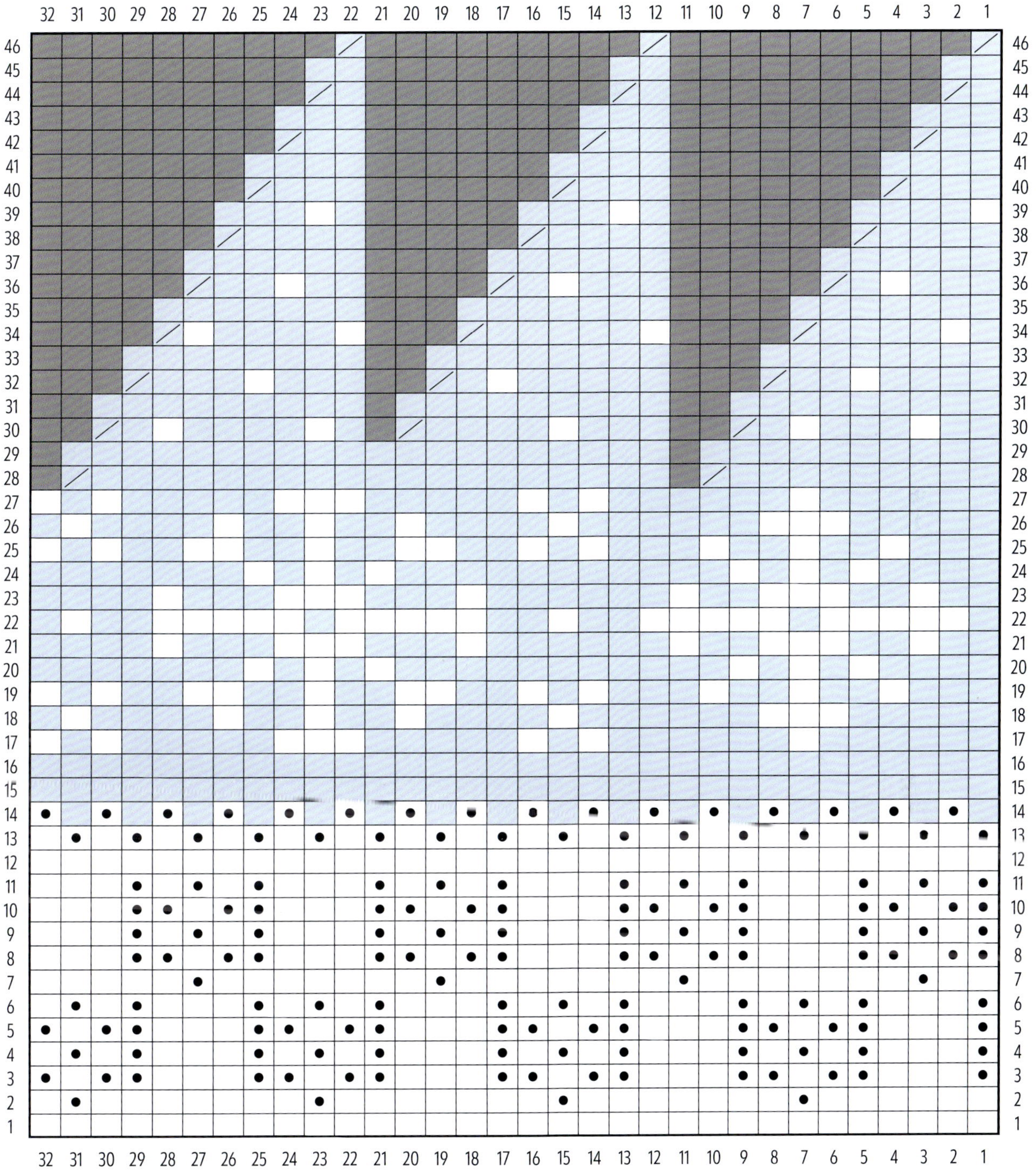

Arizona embodies everything that is classic southwest. The saguaro cactus of the Sonoran Desert, red rocks of Sedona, mining towns and ghost towns, the famous buttes of Monument Valley, and of course, the Grand Canyon are just a sampling of what makes Arizona unique. The scenery is so iconic that literally thousands of movies and TV shows have been filmed throughout the state. The topography ranges from deserts and colorful canyons to evergreen forests and mountains that are excellent for skiing. Everything from the food to the architecture seems to somehow come from a deep love of the land. The warm, rich colors of the sunsets and landscapes even carry over into fashion, home interiors, and jewelry, much of which is inspired by the beautiful beadwork and woven cloth of the Navajo people.

This design captures the warmth of Arizona in three distinct beadwork-inspired bands showcased against a turquoise backdrop, the color and name of the beloved state gemstone.

SIZE

One size fits an average adult size head (approx. 19 in. / 48 cm – 22 in. / 56 cm)

Finished Circumference: approx. 20¼ in. / 51.5 cm.

YARN

Worsted weight yarn (#4) in five colors. Shown in:

- **A:** Malabrigo Rios: Solis (50 g / 105 yd. / 96 m)
- **B:** Malabrigo Rios: Paris Night (10 g / 21 yd. / 19 m)
- **C:** Malabrigo Rios: Sunset (13 g / 27 yd./ 25 m)
- **D:** Malabrigo Rios: Natural (20 g / 42 yd. / 38 m)
- **E:** Aly Bee Workshop Merino Worsted: Honey Bee (13 g / 26 yd. / 24 m)

Continued on next page

NEEDLES

- US size 5 / 3.75 mm, 16 in. / 40 cm circular knitting needles
- US size 7 / 4.5 mm, 16 in. / 40 cm circular knitting needles
- US size 7 / 4.5 mm, set of double-pointed needles (DPNs)
- (or size needed to obtain gauge)

NOTIONS

3 stitch markers (two of one color and one of another color)

Tapestry needle for weaving in ends and working duplicate stitches

GAUGE

With larger needles, approx. 9½ stitches = 2 in. / 5 cm in stranded stockinette stitch, blocked.

Note: If you already know you are a tight knitter (or just want a larger hat), go up one or two needle sizes for both the ribbing and the body of the hat.

With smaller circular needles and color A, cast on 96 stitches. Place single color marker and join in the round, being careful not to twist stitches.

Work (k2, p2) rib pattern for approximately 1½ to 2 in. / 4 to 5 cm.

Switch to larger needles and work chart from right to left beginning on Row 1, bottom right corner. Chart repeats three times around the hat. Use remaining two stitch markers of another color to mark chart repeats.

Note: In order to avoid long "floats" (strands of yarn on the inside of the hat) and to help maintain your tension, do not carry a color more than three or four stitches without twisting the colors around each other in the back of work.

Switch to DPNs when work becomes too small for circular needles.

FINISHING

After chart is complete, cut yarn leaving a 10 in. / 25.5 cm tail. Using a tapestry needle, weave tail through remaining stitches and pull tightly to close circle. Pull tail to inside and weave in all ends.

Block as desired. See page 13 for my favorite hat blocking technique.

After all knitting and blocking is complete, work duplicate stitches where shown using a tapestry needle.

KEY

☐ K
Knit

D Dup
Work duplicate stitches after all knitting and blocking is complete.

⧄ K2tog
Knit 2 together

■ No Stitch
The "no stitch" squares represent the stitches that were lost due to decreases earlier in the round. *Do not skip a stitch.* Simply treat these squares as if they do not exist.

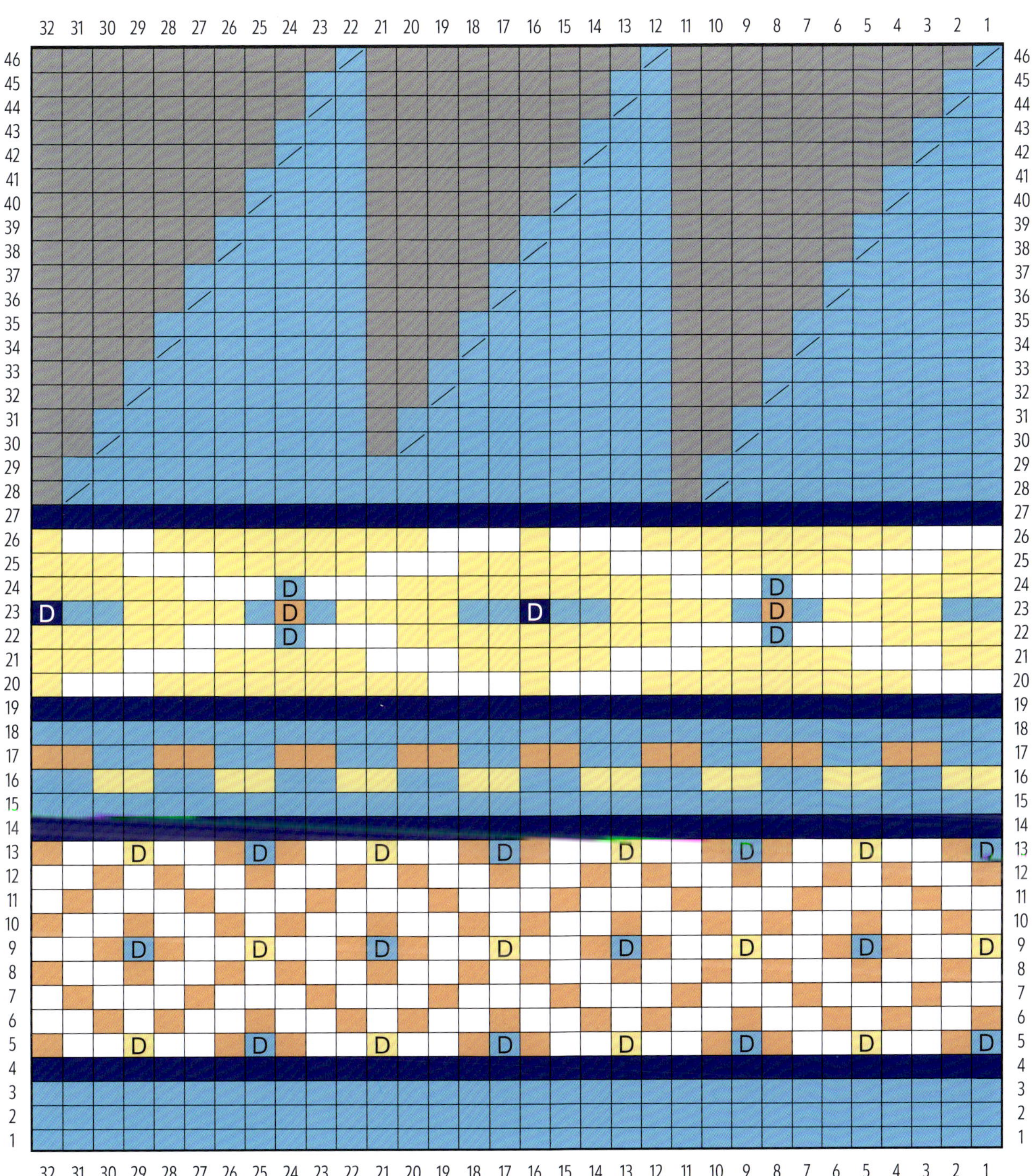

From mountains and deserts to beaches and rolling hills, the options for campers in California are an outdoor lover's dream come true. You can pitch a tent next to giant boulders, under massive pine trees, near fields of wildflowers, directly on a sandy beach, or even nestled among stately California oaks. The relatively mild weather in much of the state invites camping year-round. Although, even in the deserts, winters can get mighty chilly as soon as the sun sets—the perfect time to cozy up next to a campfire, snack on s'mores, and enjoy the beauty of the night sky.

In the subdued colors of the outdoors at night, this design features a tranquil scene of camping next to a stream and oak trees under a star-studded sky. Stars are optional.

SIZE

One size fits an average adult size head (approx. 19 in. / 48 cm – 22 in. / 56 cm)

Finished Circumference: approx. 20¼ in. / 51.5 cm.

YARN

Worsted weight yarn (#4) in five colors. Shown in:

- **A:** Aly Bee Workshop Merino Worsted: Count Chocula (25 g / 50 yd. / 46 m)
- **B:** Aly Bee Workshop Merino Worsted: Academia (10 g / 20 yd. / 18 m)
- **C:** Malabrigo Rios: Coco (20 g / 42 yd. / 38 m)
- **D:** Aly Bee Workshop Merino Worsted: Cold Brew (13 g / 26 yd. / 24 m)
- **E:** Malabrigo Rios: Azul Profundo (25 g / 52 yd. / 47 m)

Optional: A couple of yards of any color yarn for the duplicate stitched tent, tent opening, and firepit. A yard or so each of orange yarn for the campfire and white mohair for the smoke. If you choose to make more than one "campsite" you will need a little more of these colors.

Optional: Sparkly or shiny beads for the "stars."

Continued on next page

NEEDLES

- US size 5 / 3.75 mm, 16 in. / 40 cm circular knitting needles
- US size 7 / 4.5 mm, 16 in. / 40 cm circular knitting needles
- US size 7 / 4.5 mm, set of double-pointed needles (DPNs)
- (or size needed to obtain gauge)

NOTIONS

3 stitch markers (two of one color and one of another color)

Tapestry needle for weaving in ends and working duplicate stitches and embroidery

Small crochet hook or embroidery needle appropriate to the size of bead chosen for applying beads (optional)

GAUGE

With larger needles, approx. 9½ stitches = 2 in. / 5 cm in stranded stockinette stitch, blocked.

Note: If you already know you are a tight knitter (or just want a larger hat), go up one or two needle sizes for both the ribbing and the body of the hat.

With smaller circular needles and color A, cast on 96 stitches. Place single color marker and join in the round, being careful not to twist stitches.

Work (k1, p1) rib pattern for approximately 1½ to 2 in. / 4 to 5 cm.

Switch to larger needles and work chart from right to left beginning on Row 1, bottom right corner. Chart repeats three times around the hat. Use remaining two stitch markers of another color to mark chart repeats.

Note: In order to avoid long "floats" (strands of yarn on the inside of the hat) and to help maintain your tension, do not carry a color more than three or four stitches without twisting the colors around each other in the back of work. While working the trees, catching your floats behind a knit stitch rather than a purl will help minimize the amount of show through of the sky color to the front of the work.

Optional "stars": If desired, add beads to your hat to create stars in the sky. Beads can be added randomly while knitting (using the crochet hook or stringing method) or sewn on after all knitting and blocking is complete. Add as many or as few as you'd like. See photos for inspiration.

Switch to DPNs when work becomes too small for circular needles.

FINISHING

After chart is complete, cut yarn leaving a 10 in. / 25.5 cm tail. Using a tapestry needle, weave tail through remaining stitches and pull tightly to close circle. Pull tail to inside and weave in all ends.

Block as desired. See page 13 for my favorite hat blocking technique.

Add tent and campfire: After all knitting and blocking is complete, work duplicate stitches where shown using a tapestry needle and any desired color for your tent and firepit. Add campfire and smoke with straight stitches. See photos for inspiration.

KEY

- ☐ **K** — Knit
- D **Dup** — Work duplicate stitches after all knitting and blocking is complete.
- • **P** — Purl
- V **S1** — Slip one purlwise with yarn in back
- / **K2tog** — Knit 2 together
- ■ **No Stitch** — The "no stitch" squares represent the stitches that were lost due to decreases earlier in the round. *Do not skip a stitch.* Simply treat these squares as if they do not exist.

32 31 30 29 28 27 26 25 24 23 22 21 20 19 18 17 16 15 14 13 12 11 10 9 8 7 6 5 4 3 2 1

45 44 43 42 41 40 39 38 37 36 35 34 33 32 31 30 29 28 27 26 25 24 23 22 21 20 19 18 17 16 15 14 13 12 11 10 9 8 7 6 5 4 3 2 1

32 31 30 29 28 27 26 25 24 23 22 21 20 19 18 17 16 15 14 13 12 11 10 9 8 7 6 5 4 3 2 1

It's almost impossible to think about Colorado without thinking about mountains. With a varied topography of high plains, valleys, canyons, and plateaus, the entire state sits above an elevation of three thousand feet. Dominating almost half of the landscape are the famous Rocky Mountains (running nearly down the center) that create some of the state's most famous and wondrous features, including more than fifty peaks above fourteen thousand feet. With opportunities for endless year-round outdoor adventures, spectacular scenic drives, several historic railroads, four national parks, and big cities and small towns galore, Colorado attracts tourists and adventurers from around the country and around the world.

Inspired by the flora and fauna of the Rocky Mountains, this design features elk, evergreen trees, and aspen groves with snow-topped mountain peaks in the distance.

SIZE

One size fits an average adult size head (approx. 19 in. / 48 cm – 22 in. / 56 cm)

Finished Circumference: approx. 20¼ in. / 51.5 cm.

YARN

- **A:** Malabrigo Rios: Sandstorm (50 g / 105 yd. / 96 m)
- **B:** Malabrigo Rios: Natural (50 g / 105 yd. / 96 m)

Note: The above amounts will allow enough for an optional pom-pom.

Alternate version: Using whatever appropriate colors you have on hand, use the same chart to make a "colorized" version of this design. Add the pine and aspen trees using duplicate stitches.

Continued on next page

NEEDLES

- US size 5 / 3.75 mm, 16 in. / 40 cm circular knitting needles
- US size 7 / 4.5 mm, 16 in. / 40 cm circular knitting needles
- US size 7 / 4.5 mm, set of double-pointed needles (DPNs) (or size needed to obtain gauge)

NOTIONS

3 stitch markers (two of one color and one of another color)

Tapestry needle for weaving in ends.

GAUGE

With larger needles, approx. 9½ stitches = 2 in. / 5 cm in stranded stockinette stitch, blocked.

Note: If you already know you are a tight knitter (or just want a larger hat), go up one or two needle sizes for both the ribbing and the body of the hat.

With smaller circular needles and color B, cast on 96 stitches. Place single color marker and join in the round, being careful not to twist stitches.

Work (k2, p2) rib pattern for approximately 1½ to 2 in. / 4 to 5 cm.

Switch to larger needles and work chart from right to left beginning on Row 1, bottom right corner. Chart repeats three times around the hat. Use remaining two stitch markers of another color to mark chart repeats.

Note: In order to avoid long "floats" (strands of yarn on the inside of the hat) and to help maintain your tension, do not carry a color more than three or four stitches without twisting the colors around each other in the back of work.

Switch to DPNs when work becomes too small for circular needles.

FINISHING

After chart is complete, cut yarn leaving a 10 in. / 25.5 cm tail. Using a tapestry needle, weave tail through remaining stitches and pull tightly to close circle. Pull tail to inside and weave in all ends.

Optional: Using your favorite method, make a pom-pom and attach to top of hat.

Block as desired. See page 13 for my favorite hat blocking technique.

KEY

☐ K
Knit

☑ S1
Slip one purlwise with yarn in back

⧄ K2tog
Knit 2 together

■ No Stitch
The "no stitch" squares represent the stitches that were lost due to decreases earlier in the round. *Do not skip a stitch.* Simply treat these squares as if they do not exist.

⧅ SSK
Slip, slip, knit: Slip 2 stitches knitwise, return both to left needle and knit slipped stitches together through back loop

32 31 30 29 28 27 26 25 24 23 22 21 20 19 18 17 16 15 14 13 12 11 10 9 8 7 6 5 4 3 2 1

46 45 44 43 42 41 40 39 38 37 36 35 34 33 32 31 30 29 28 27 26 25 24 23 22 21 20 19 18 17 16 15 14 13 12 11 10 9 8 7 6 5 4 3 2 1

32 31 30 29 28 27 26 25 24 23 22 21 20 19 18 17 16 15 14 13 12 11 10 9 8 7 6 5 4 3 2 1

Color and Hawaii go hand in hand. From the abundance of flowers, grasses, and trees that flourish on the land to red-hot lava, beautiful blue skies, and ocean that surround the state—color is everywhere! Hawaiians have always embraced the colors of this amazing place. You see it in traditional and modern clothing, in jewelry and paintings, in songs, and of course, in all the beautiful flower leis and headpieces. Whether worn in traditional dances at luaus and other celebrations or simply by enthusiastic tourists with a love of the culture, leis are an iconic symbol of Hawaiian hospitality. But did you know that each of the eight Hawaiian Islands has its own official color? The chosen colors represent the different flowers found on each island: red, orange, pink, yellow, gray, white, green, and purple. Can you match the color to the island?

Featuring an orchid lei and tropical flowers, this design incorporates the colors of all eight islands, as well as the beautiful blue ocean that binds them together.

SIZE

One size fits an average adult size head (approx. 19 in. / 48 cm – 22 in. / 56 cm)

Finished Circumference: approx. 20¼ in. / 51.5 cm.

YARN

Worsted weight yarn (#4) in nine colors. Shown in:

- **A:** Ewe 2 Yarn Mellow Worsted: Breeze (33 g / 72 yd. / 66 m)
- **B:** Aly Bee Workshop Merino Worsted: Spooky (5 g / 10 yd. / 9 m)
- **C:** Aly Bee Workshop Merino Worsted: Cindersnap (20 g / 40 yd. / 37 m)
- **D:** Aly Bee Workshop Merino Worsted: Nebula (15 g / 30 yd. / 27 m)
- **E:** Malabrigo Rios: Natural (5 g / 11 yd. / 10 m)
- **F:** Aly Bee Workshop Merino Worsted: Limoncello (5 g / 10 yd. / 9 m)
- **G:** Stunning String Studio Legacy Worsted: Zinfandel (10 g / 21 yd. / 19 m)
- **H:** *Aly Bee Workshop Merino Worsted: Marmalade (5 g / 11 yd. / 10 m)
- **I:** *Aly Bee Workshop Merino Worsted: Festive (2–3 yd. / 1.75–2.75 m)

*Used only in duplicate stitching

Continued on next page

NEEDLES

- US size 5 / 3.75 mm, 16 in. / 40 cm circular knitting needles
- US size 7 / 4.5 mm, 16 in. / 40 cm circular knitting needles
- US size 7 / 4.5 mm, set of double-pointed needles (DPNs)
- (or size needed to obtain gauge)

NOTIONS

3 stitch markers (two of one color and one of another color)

Tapestry needle for weaving in ends and working duplicate stitches

GAUGE

With larger needles, approx. 9½ stitches = 2 in. / 5 cm in stranded stockinette stitch, blocked.

Note: If you already know you are a tight knitter (or just want a larger hat), go up one or two needle sizes for both the ribbing and the body of the hat.

With smaller circular needles and color A, cast on 96 stitches. Place single color marker and join in the round, being careful not to twist stitches.

Work (k1, p1) rib pattern for approximately 1½ to 2 in. / 4 to 5 cm.

Switch to larger needles and work chart from right to left beginning on Row 1, bottom right corner. Chart repeats three times around the hat. Use remaining two stitch markers of another color to mark chart repeats.

Note: In order to avoid long "floats" (strands of yarn on the inside of the hat) and to help maintain your tension, do not carry a color more than three or four stitches without twisting the colors around each other in the back of work.

Switch to DPNs when work becomes too small for circular needles.

FINISHING

After chart is complete, cut yarn leaving a 10 in. / 25.5 cm tail. Using a tapestry needle, weave tail through remaining stitches and pull tightly to close circle. Pull tail to inside and weave in all ends.

Block as desired. See page 13 for my favorite hat blocking technique.

After all knitting and blocking is complete, work duplicate stitches to add details to flowers in colors and locations shown using a tapestry needle.

KEY

☐ K
Knit

D Dup
Work duplicate stitches after all knitting and blocking is complete.

⧄ K2tog
Knit 2 together

■ No Stitch
The "no stitch" squares represent the stitches that were lost due to decreases earlier in the round. *Do not skip a stitch*. Simply treat these squares as if they do not exist.

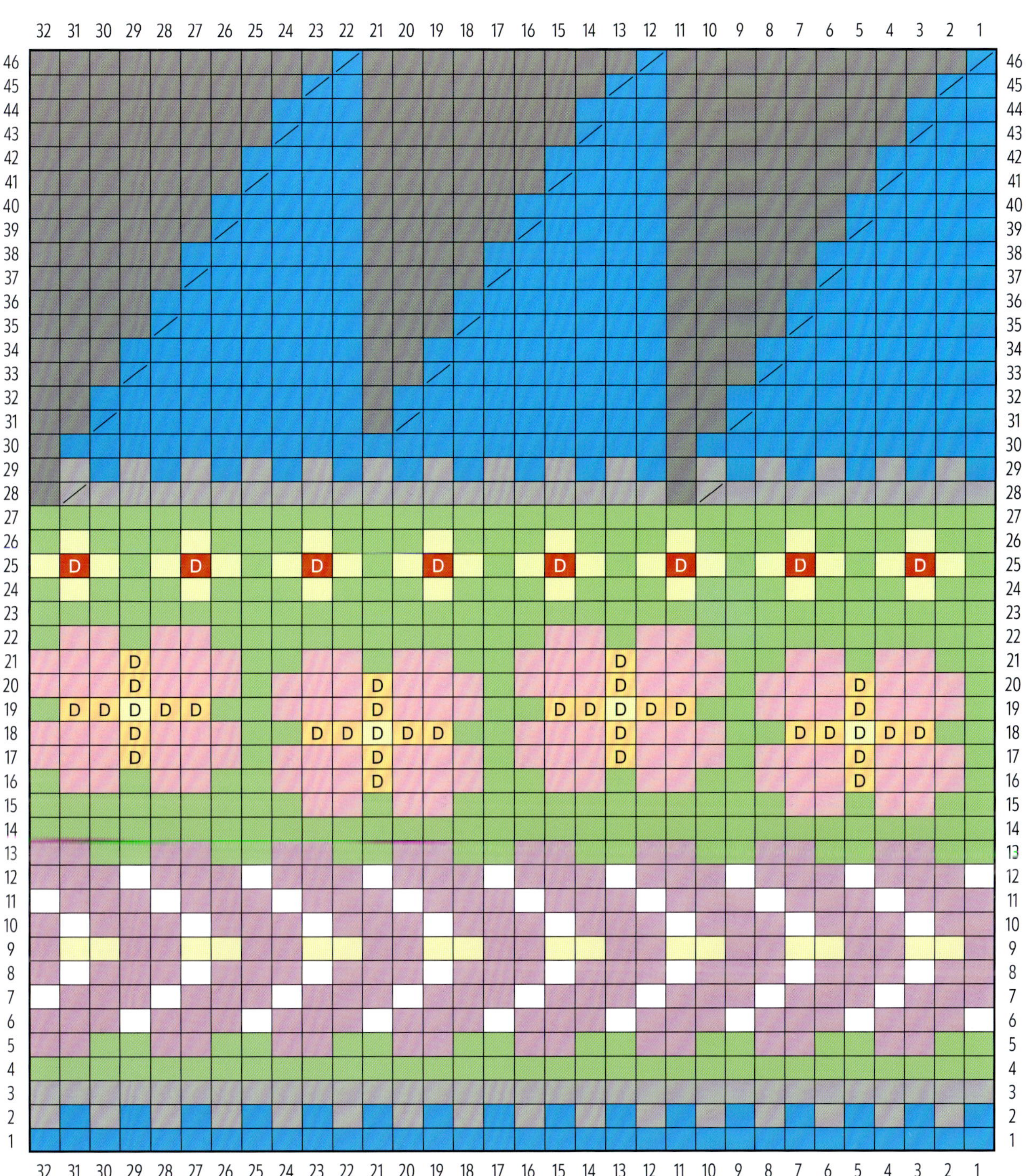

It's not hard to guess how the Sawtooth Range of Idaho got its name. This jagged and magnificent range (part of the Rocky Mountains) contains an astounding fifty-seven peaks over ten thousand feet of elevation! And it just happens to resemble an old handsaw. Hundreds of pristine lakes and rivers beckon to boaters, fishermen, kayakers, and rafters looking for adventures with a beautiful view. The massive peaks call to the rock and mountain climbers while the trails and campgrounds invite hikers, backpackers, campers, and casual picnickers to soak in the fresh air and wildlife viewing. And the dark skies offer amazing stargazing and a clear view of the Milky Way to anyone who is lucky enough to look up.

This design features jagged peaks and tall evergreens reflected in a mountain lake. Wild huckleberries on the bushes in the foreground are ripe for the picking!

SIZE

One size fits an average adult size head (approx. 19 in. / 48 cm – 22 in. / 56 cm)

Finished Circumference: approx. 20¼ in. / 51.5 cm.

YARN

Worsted weight yarn (#4) in five colors. Shown in:

- **A:** Stunning String Studio Legacy Worsted: Pine Bough (40 g / 86 yd. / 79 m)
- **B:** Polka Dot Sheep Whitefish Worsted: Tally Lake (20 g / 44 yd. / 40 m)
- **C:** Stunning String Studio Legacy Worsted: Calypso Blu (15 g / 32 yd. / 29 m)
- **D:** Seismic Yarn & Dyeworks Butter Worsted: Petrified (20 g / 44 yd. / 40 m)
- **E:** Stunning String Studio Legacy Worsted: Something Blue (15 g / 32 yd. / 29 m)

Optional: 5–8 yards of a purple/blue color to add huckleberries to the bushes. I used Polka Dot Sheep Whitefish Worsted in Huckleberry. See photo for inspiration.

Continued on next page

NEEDLES

- US size 5 / 3.75 mm, 16 in. / 40 cm circular knitting needles
- US size 7 / 4.5 mm, 16 in. / 40 cm circular knitting needles
- US size 7 / 4.5 mm, set of double-pointed needles (DPNs)
- (or size needed to obtain gauge)

NOTIONS

3 stitch markers (two of one color and one of another color)

Tapestry needle for weaving in ends and working embroidery

GAUGE

With larger needles, approx. 9½ stitches = 2 in. / 5 cm in stranded stockinette stitch, blocked.

Note: If you already know you are a tight knitter (or just want a larger hat), go up one or two needle sizes for both the ribbing and the body of the hat.

With smaller circular needles and color A, cast on 96 stitches. Place single color marker and join in the round, being careful not to twist stitches.

Work in (k1, p1) rib pattern for approximately 4 in. / 10 cm for a fold-over ribbing/brim as shown or approximately 1½ to 2 in. / 4 to 5 cm for a single layer ribbing.

Switch to larger needles and work chart from right to left beginning on Row 1, bottom right corner. Chart repeats three times around the hat.

Use remaining two stitch markers of another color to mark chart repeats.

Note: In order to avoid long "floats" (strands of yarn on the inside of the hat) and to help maintain your tension, do not carry a color more than three or four stitches without twisting the colors around each other in the back of work.

Switch to DPNs when work becomes too small for circular needles.

FINISHING

After chart is complete, cut yarn leaving a 10 in. / 25.5 cm tail. Using a tapestry needle, weave tail through remaining stitches and pull tightly to close circle. Pull tail to inside and weave in all ends.

Block as desired. See page 13 for my favorite hat blocking technique.

Optional: Add French knot "huckleberries" to the bushes. I used only 2 strands of the 4-ply yarn to make smaller French knots. Placement is random in Rows 2-4. Add as many or as few as you'd like. See photo for inspiration.

KEY

☐ K
Knit

☑ S1
Slip one purlwise with yarn in back

⧄ K2tog
Knit 2 together

■ No Stitch
The "no stitch" squares represent the stitches that were lost due to decreases earlier in the round. *Do not skip a stitch.* Simply treat these squares as if they do not exist.

Montana really does have big skies! What started out as an ad campaign using the title of a book, the Big Sky State stuck as the unofficial nickname of Montana, perfectly describing the nearly unobstructed views of vast grasslands and prairies in the eastern half of the state. In stark contrast, the Rocky Mountains cut through the western half of the state, creating spectacular alpine forests, glaciers, lakes, rivers, mountain peaks, and meadows, especially in picturesque Glacier National Park near the northernmost border of the state. The world famous Going-to-the-Sun Road is one of the best ways to see this amazing landscape. In a state with the most grizzlies in the lower forty-eight and where cows outnumber humans, you'll also find great food, fascinating history, a rich Native American and cattle-ranching culture, and a powerful sense of community. Even the bigger cities somehow have a small-town vibe.

Wild Montana skies and cattle ranching feature *big* in this design. With or without the optional cattle, the scene is classic Montana.

SIZE

One size fits an average adult size head (approx. 19 in. / 48 cm – 22 in. / 56 cm)

Finished Circumference: approx. 20¼ in. / 51.5 cm.

YARN

Worsted weight yarn (#4) in five colors. Shown in:

- **A:** Stunning String Studio Legacy Worsted: Rosemary (40 g / 86 yd. / 79 m)
- **B:** Malabrigo Rios: Black* (5 g / 10 yd. / 9 m)
- **C:** Stunning String Studio Legacy Worsted: Big Sky (33 g / 71 yd. / 65 m)
- **D:** Stunning String Studio Legacy Worsted: Dove (15 g / 32 yd. / 29 m)
- **E:** Aly Bee Workshop Merino Worsted: Vanilla (20 g / 40 yd. / 37 m)

*__Note:__ If you decide not to add cattle to your design, simply leave out the black stitches and knit the entire grasslands in color A.

Continued on next page

NEEDLES

- US size 5 / 3.75 mm, 16 in. / 40 cm circular knitting needles
- US size 7 / 4.5 mm, 16 in. / 40 cm circular knitting needles
- US size 7 / 4.5 mm, set of double-pointed needles (DPNs)
- (or size needed to obtain gauge)

NOTIONS

3 stitch markers (two of one color and one of another color)

Tapestry needle for weaving in ends

GAUGE

With larger needles, approx. 9½ stitches = 2 in. / 5 cm in stranded stockinette stitch, blocked.

Note: If you already know you are a tight knitter (or just want a larger hat), go up one or two needle sizes for both the ribbing and the body of the hat.

With smaller circular needles and color A, cast on 96 stitches. Place single color marker and join in the round, being careful not to twist stitches.

Work (k2, p2) rib pattern for approximately 4 in. / 10 cm for a fold-over ribbing/brim as shown or approximately 1½ to 2 in. / 4 to 5 cm. for a single layer ribbing.

Switch to larger needles and work chart from right to left beginning on Row 1, bottom right corner. Chart repeats three times around the hat.

Use remaining two stitch markers of another color to mark chart repeats.

Note: In order to avoid long "floats" (strands of yarn on the inside of the hat) and to help maintain your tension, do not carry a color more than three or four stitches without twisting the colors around each other in the back of work.

Switch to DPNs when work becomes too small for circular needles.

FINISHING

After chart is complete, cut yarn leaving a 10 in. / 25.5 cm tail. Using a tapestry needle, weave tail through remaining stitches and pull tightly to close circle. Pull tail to inside and weave in all ends.

Block as desired. See page 13 for my favorite hat blocking technique.

KEY

☐ K
Knit

☑ S1
Slip one purlwise with yarn in back

⧄ K2tog
Knit 2 together

■ No Stitch
The "no stitch" squares represent the stitches that were lost due to decreases earlier in the round. *Do not skip a stitch.* Simply treat these squares as if they do not exist.

Less than fifty miles outside the glow of the lights of Las Vegas lie forty thousand acres of bright red and orange sandstone formations so vivid, they seem to create a natural glow of their own: Valley of Fire State Park. From nearly white to dark red, the layers of color and intricate formations created by time, wind, and water are seemingly endless and utterly fascinating. From stone arches and slot canyons to abstract sculpted formations and large smooth surfaces that resemble bacon, this park is a geologic wonder just waiting to be explored.

In predominantly warm tones, the famous Fire Wave formation takes center stage in this design against a backdrop of red sandstone cliffs in the glow of sunset.

SIZE

One size fits an average adult size head (approx. 19 in. / 48 cm – 22 in. / 56 cm)

Finished Circumference: approx. 20¼ in. / 51.5 cm.

YARN

Worsted weight yarn (#4) in four colors. Shown in:

- **A:** Peekaboo Yarns Merino Worsted: Yam (20 g / 44 yd. / 40 m)
- **B:** Aly Bee Workshop Merino Worsted: Kettlecorn (20 g / 40 yd. / 37 m)
- **C:** Aly Bee Workshop Merino Worsted: Farmhouse (40 g / 80 yd. / 73 m)
- **D:** Malabrigo Rios: Sunset (15 g / 32 yd. / 29 m)

NEEDLES

- US size 5 / 3.75 mm, 16 in. / 40 cm circular knitting needles
- US size 7 / 4.5 mm, 16 in. / 40 cm circular knitting needles
- US size 7 / 4.5 mm, set of double-pointed needles (DPNs)
- (or size needed to obtain gauge)

Continued on next page

NOTIONS

3 stitch markers (two of one color and one of another color)

Tapestry needle for weaving in ends and working duplicate stitches

GAUGE

With larger needles, approx. 9½ stitches = 2 in. / 5 cm in stranded stockinette stitch, blocked.

Note: If you already know you are a tight knitter (or just want a larger hat), go up one or two needle sizes for both the ribbing and the body of the hat.

With smaller circular needles and color C, cast on 96 stitches. Place single color marker and join in the round, being careful not to twist stitches.

Work (k1 tbl, p1) rib pattern for approximately 1½ to 2 in. / 4 to 5 cm. (tbl=through back loop)

Switch to larger needles and work chart from right to left beginning on Row 1, bottom right corner. Chart repeats three times around the hat. Use remaining two stitch markers of another color to mark chart repeats.

Note: In order to avoid long "floats" (strands of yarn on the inside of the hat) and to help maintain your tension, do not carry a color more than three or four stitches without twisting the colors around each other in the back of work.

Switch to DPNs when work becomes too small for circular needles.

FINISHING

After chart is complete, cut yarn leaving a 10 in. / 25.5 cm tail. Using a tapestry needle, weave tail through remaining stitches and pull tightly to close circle. Pull tail to inside and weave in all ends.

Block as desired. See page 13 for my favorite hat blocking technique.

After all knitting and blocking is complete, work duplicate stitches where shown using a tapestry needle.

KEY

- ☐ K — Knit
- D Dup — Work duplicate stitches after all knitting and blocking is complete.
- • P — Purl
- K-tbl — Knit through back loop
- / K2tog — Knit 2 together
- ■ No Stitch — The "no stitch" squares represent the stitches that were lost due to decreases earlier in the round. *Do not skip a stitch.* Simply treat these squares as if they do not exist.
- V S1 — Slip one purlwise with yarn in back

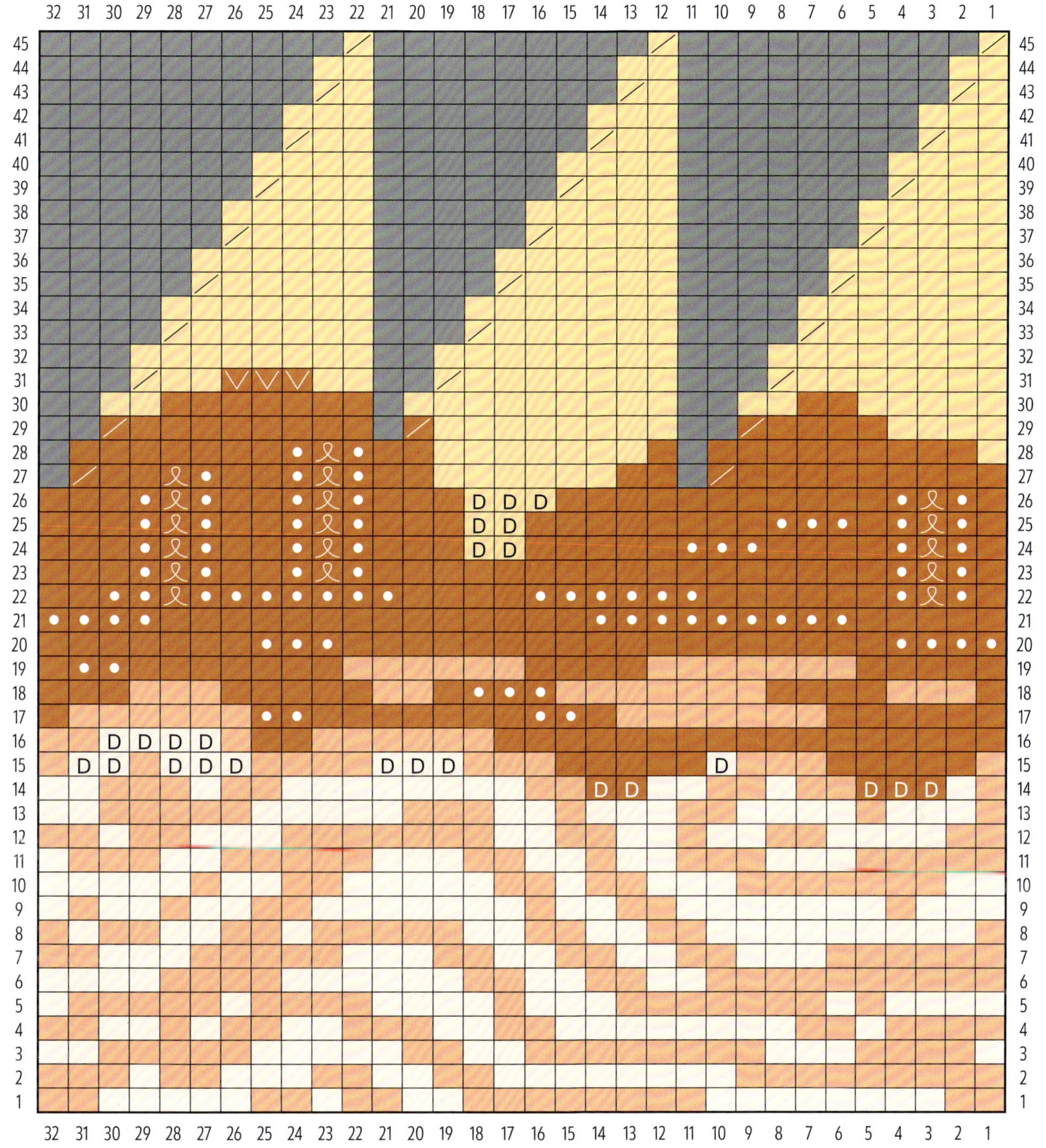

SIZE

One size fits an average adult size head (approx. 19 in. / 48 cm – 22 in. / 56 cm)

Finished Circumference: approx. 20¼ in. / 51.5 cm.

YARN

Worsted weight yarn (#4) in three colors. Shown in:

A: (not shown on chart) Polka Dot Sheep Whitefish Worsted: Moose Meadow (20 g / 44 yd. / 40 m)

B: Aly Bee Workshop Merino Worsted: Marble Soda (33 g/ 66 yd./ 60 m)

C: Polka Dot Sheep Whitefish Worsted: Tulip Festival (33 g / 72 yd. / 66 m)

NEEDLES

- US size 5 / 3.75 mm, 16 in. / 40 cm circular knitting needles
- US size 7 / 4.5 mm, 16 in. / 40 cm circular knitting needles
- US size 7 / 4.5 mm, set of double-pointed needles (DPNs)
- (or size needed to obtain gauge)

Continued on next page

A ride in a hot air balloon is a bucket list item for so many people, and New Mexico is a great place to check that one off the list. Perhaps it's the idea of floating through the sky, enjoying panoramic views without the need for a noisy airplane, that draws us to ballooning. Or the feeling of weightlessness or floating on a cloud. Whatever the reason, the annual Albuquerque International Balloon Fiesta (the largest ballooning event in the world) is the perfect opportunity to fulfill that dream. Even if you'd rather watch from the ground, a balloon-filled sky is an unforgettable sight. For the more earthbound adventurers, New Mexico is also home to cliff dwellings, a scenic railroad, a UFO museum, spectacular vistas, amazing food, petroglyphs, two national parks, and so much more. No wonder it's nicknamed the Land of Enchantment.

Colorful balloons fill a bright-blue sky in this design. The largest balloon is reminiscent of vintage balloons covered in netting. It might not be a bucket list item, but knitting a hot air balloon? Check!

NOTIONS

3 stitch markers (two of one color and one of another color)

Tapestry needle for weaving in ends

GAUGE

With larger needles, approx. 9½ stitches = 2 in. / 5 cm in stranded stockinette stitch, blocked.

Note: If you already know you are a tight knitter (or just want a larger hat), go up one or two needle sizes for both the ribbing and the body of the hat.

Switch to DPNs when work becomes too small for circular needles.

FINISHING

After chart is complete, cut yarn leaving a 10 in. / 25.5 cm tail. Using a tapestry needle, weave tail through remaining stitches and pull tightly to close circle. Pull tail to inside and weave in all ends.

Block as desired. See page 13 for my favorite hat blocking technique.

KEY

☐ K
Knit

⧄ K2tog
Knit 2 together

■ No Stitch
The "no stitch" squares represent the stitches that were lost due to decreases earlier in the round. *Do not skip a stitch.* Simply treat these squares as if they do not exist.

With smaller circular needles and color A, cast on 96 stitches. Place single color marker and join in the round, being careful not to twist stitches.

Work (k1, p1) rib pattern for approximately 1½ to 2 in. / 4 to 5 cm.

Switch to larger needles and work chart from right to left beginning on Row 1, bottom right corner. Chart repeats three times around the hat. Use remaining two stitch markers of another color to mark chart repeats.

Note: In order to avoid long "floats" (strands of yarn on the inside of the hat) and to help maintain your tension, do not carry a color more than three or four stitches without twisting the colors around each other in the back of work.

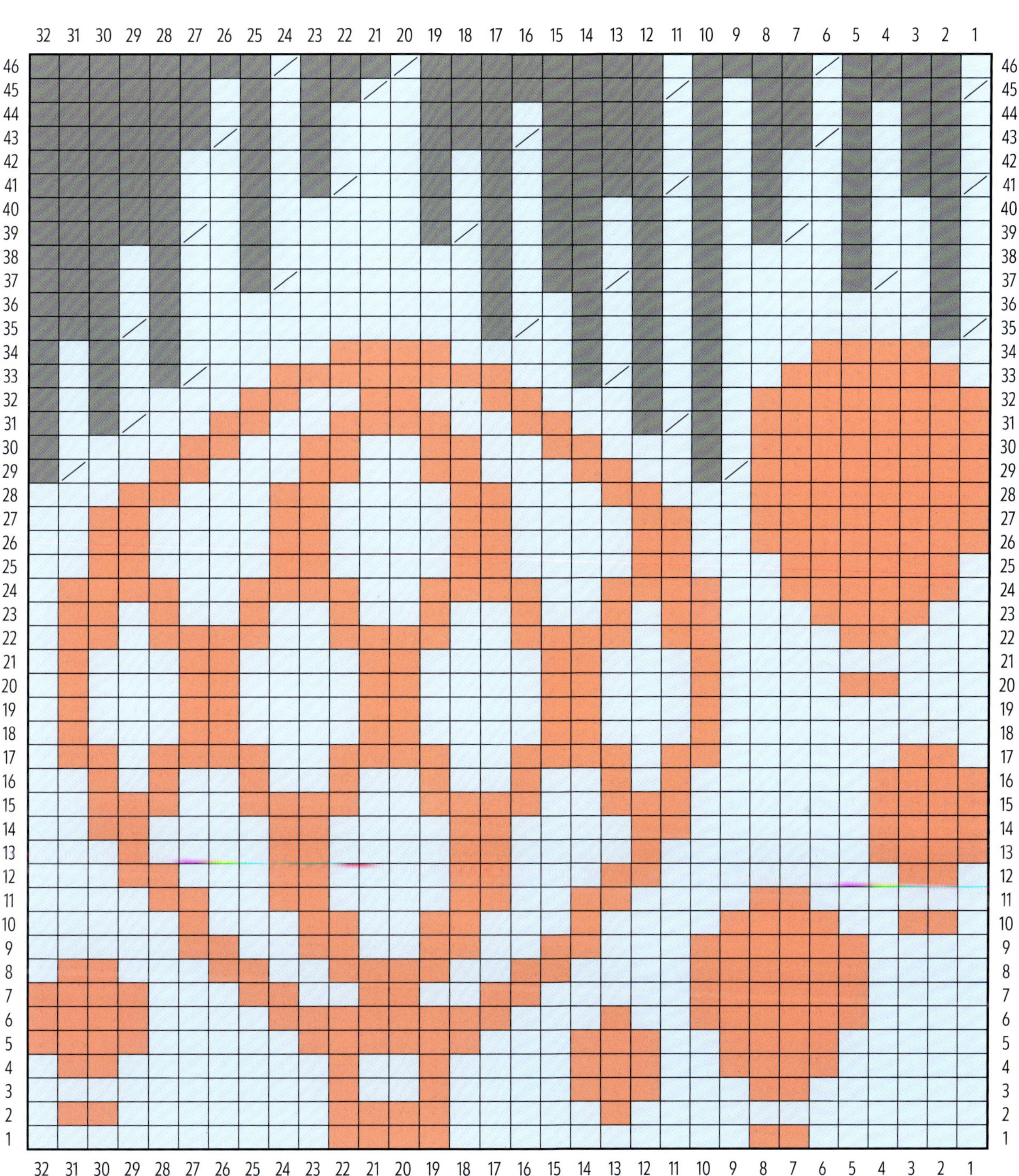

The waterfalls, forested mountains, lakes, streams, and iron-rich red soil often come as a surprise to folks visiting Oklahoma for the first time. Understandably so! What comes to mind first is usually the vast golden plains and prairies with gently rolling hills that dominate most of the landscape. Add in a few herds of bison or cattle, and the classic Oklahoma scene is complete. From a history standpoint, Oklahoma is rich in Native American culture, cattle ranching, and agriculture, as well as oil and natural gas production. But it also boasts one of the longest drivable stretches of the iconic Route 66 and an abundance of rose rock, the official state rock of Oklahoma. This fascinating flower-shaped rock formed by barite crystals is found in very few places in the world.

This easy-to-knit design captures the spirit of the iconic Oklahoma landscape from a lake lined with shrubbery on one side to the red dirt embedded with rose rocks on the other. Golden prairies (with optional oil derricks) under a sunny sky complete the scene.

SIZE

One size fits an average adult size head (approx. 19 in. / 48 cm – 22 in. / 56 cm)

Finished Circumference: approx. 20¼ in. / 51.5 cm.

YARN

Worsted weight yarn (#4) in seven colors. Shown in:

- **A:** Malabrigo Rios: Ivy (20 g/ 42 yd./ 38 m)
- **B:** Stunning String Studio Legacy Worsted: Storm Cloud (10 g / 21 yd. / 19 m)
- **C:** Aly Bee Workshop Merino Worsted: Farmhouse (10 g / 20 yd. / 18 m)
- **D:** Peekaboo Yarns Merino Worsted: Yam (10 g / 21 yd. / 19 m)
- **E:** Stunning String Studio Legacy Worsted: Desert Floor (15 g / 32 yd. / 29 m)
- **F:** Aly Bee Workshop Merino Worsted: Glass Slipper (20 g / 40 yd. / 37 m)
- **G:** Malabrigo Rios: Natural (10 g / 21 yd. / 19 m)

Optional: A few yards of black yarn for embroidering oil derrick/pump on the prairie.

Continued on next page

NEEDLES

- US size 5 / 3.75 mm, 16 in. / 40 cm circular knitting needles
- US size 7 / 4.5 mm, 16 in. / 40 cm circular knitting needles
- US size 7 / 4.5 mm, set of double-pointed needles (DPNs)
- (or size needed to obtain gauge)

NOTIONS

3 stitch markers (two of one color and one of another color)

Tapestry needle for weaving in ends and working embroidery

GAUGE

With larger needles, approx. 9½ stitches = 2 in. / 5 cm in stranded stockinette stitch, blocked.

Note: If you already know you are a tight knitter (or just want a larger hat), go up one or two needle sizes for both the ribbing and the body of the hat.

With smaller circular needles and color A, cast on 96 stitches. Place single color marker and join in the round, being careful not to twist stitches.

Work (k1, p1) rib pattern for approximately 1½ to 2 in. / 4 to 5 cm.

Switch to larger needles and work chart from right to left beginning on Row 1, bottom right corner. Chart repeats three times around the hat. Use remaining two stitch markers of another color to mark chart repeats.

Note: In order to avoid long "floats" (strands of yarn on the inside of the hat) and to help maintain your tension, do not carry a color more than three or four stitches without twisting the colors around each other in the back of work.

Switch to DPNs when work becomes too small for circular needles.

FINISHING

After chart is complete, cut yarn leaving a 10 in. / 25.5 cm tail. Using a tapestry needle, weave tail through remaining stitches and pull tightly to close circle. Pull tail to inside and weave in all ends.

Block as desired. See page 13 for my favorite hat blocking technique.

Optional embroidery: After all blocking is complete, with tapestry needle and black yarn, add oil derricks and/or pumps to the prairie using simple straight stitches. I separated the 4 plies of yarn and used only 2 plies for the cross braces of the derrick and 4 plies for everything else. See photo for inspiration.

KEY

- ☐ K — Knit
- ⊡ P — Purl
- ☑ S1 — Slip one purlwise with yarn in back
- ⧄ K2tog — Knit 2 together
- ■ No Stitch — The "no stitch" squares represent the stitches that were lost due to decreases earlier in the round. *Do not skip a stitch.* Simply treat these squares as if they do not exist.

From forests, farmlands, and vineyards to raging rivers and spectacular canyons, there's much to be said about the beauty of Oregon. But perhaps the most standout feature of this gorgeous Pacific Northwest state is the waterfalls. With nearly 240 known waterfalls, you'll find falls you can hike to, bike to, view from the top or the bottom of (or even from the road), swim near, and camp next to—and some you can even walk behind. Many are tall and narrow, such as the 620-foot Multnomah Falls, the tallest in the state, while others are wide and short, such as Willamette Falls at 1,500 feet wide and 42 feet tall. Some are easy to get to via short, paved paths while others require a more adventurous route. Whatever your favorite waterfall style, you'll surely find it in Oregon.

Using a single water-inspired color and a variety of cable stitches, wide and narrow asymmetrical waterfalls tumble and splash into the rivers (the ribbing) in this fun and stylized interpretation. Randomly placed mini bobbles add to the appearance of churning water.

SIZE

One size fits an average adult size head (approx. 19 in. / 48 cm – 22 in. / 56 cm)

Finished Circumference: approx. 20¼ in. / 51.5 cm.

YARN

Worsted weight yarn (#4) in one color. Shown in:

A: Polka Dot Sheep Whitefish Worsted: Mystic (100 g / 218 yd. / 199 m)

NEEDLES

- US size 5 / 3.75 mm, 16 in. / 40 cm circular knitting needles
- US size 7 / 4.5 mm, 16 in. / 40 cm circular knitting needles
- US size 7 / 4.5 mm, set of double-pointed needles (DPNs)
- (or size needed to obtain gauge)

Continued on next page

NOTIONS

3 stitch markers (two of one color and one of another color)

Tapestry needle for weaving in ends

Cable needle (CN)

GAUGE

With larger needles, approx. 9½ stitches = 2 in. / 5 cm in stranded stockinette stitch, blocked.

Note: If you already know you are a tight knitter (or just want a larger hat), go up one or two needle sizes for both the ribbing and the body of the hat.

With smaller circular needles, cast on 96 stitches. Place single color marker and join in the round, being careful not to twist stitches.

Work (k1, p1) rib pattern for approximately 1½ to 2 in. / 4 to 5 cm.

Optional: Add more "splashes" to the waterfall pools with additional bobbles worked IN the ribbing. In the last 2–3 rows of ribbing (and in the increase row), add a few randomly placed mini-bobbles under the waterfalls. This brings the "splashing" down *into* the ribbing.

Increase Round: *K31, kfb; repeat from * 2 more times - 99 sts total.

Switch to larger needles and work chart from right to left beginning on Row 1, bottom right corner. Chart repeats three times around the hat. Use remaining two stitch markers of another color to mark chart repeats.

Switch to DPNs when work becomes too small for circular needles.

FINISHING

After chart is complete, cut yarn leaving a 10 in. / 25.5 cm tail. Using a tapestry needle, weave tail through remaining stitches and pull tightly to close circle. Pull tail to inside and weave in all ends.

Block as desired. See page 13 for my favorite hat blocking technique.

Stitch Key: The colors shown are merely to help identify the various cable stitches on the chart. The entire design is knit in one color.

KEY

K
Knit

Mb
Mini bobble: (p1, k1, p1, k1) into next stitch, then lift 2nd, 3rd, and 4th stitches over first stitch and off needle, one at a time.

P
Purl

2/1 RPC
Slip 1 stitch to cable needle and hold in back; k2; p1 from cable needle.

3/1 LPC
Slip 3 stitches to cable needle and hold in front; p1; k3 from cable needle.

3/3 LC
Slip 3 stitches to cable needle and hold in front; k3; k3 from cable needle.

3/1 RPC
Slip 1 stitch to cable needle and hold in back; k3; p1 from cable needle.

2/3 RC
Slip 3 stitches to cable needle and hold in back; k2; k3 from cable needle.

3/2 LC
Slip 3 stitches to cable needle and hold in front; k2; k3 from cable needle.

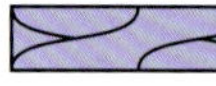

3/3 RC
Slip 3 stitches to cable needle and hold in back; k3; k3 from cable needle.

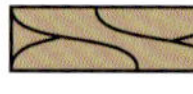

2/3 LC
Slip 2 stitches to cable needle and hold in front; k3; k2 from cable needle.

3/2 RC
Slip 2 stitches to cable needle and hold in back; k3; k2 from cable needle..

2/1 LPC
Slip 2 stitches to cable needle and hold in front; p1; k2 from cable needle.

3/2 RPC
Slip 2 stitches to cable needle and hold in back; k3; p2 from cable needle.

P2tog
Purl 2 together

No Stitch
The "no stitch" squares represent the stitches that were lost due to decreases earlier in the round. *Do not skip a stitch*. Simply treat these squares as if they do not exist.

ssk
Slip, slip, knit: Slip 2 stitches knitwise, place stitches back on left needle, knit 2 tog through back loop

K2tog
Knit 2 together

2/2 LC
Slip 2 stitches to cable needle and hold in front; k2; k2 from cable needle.

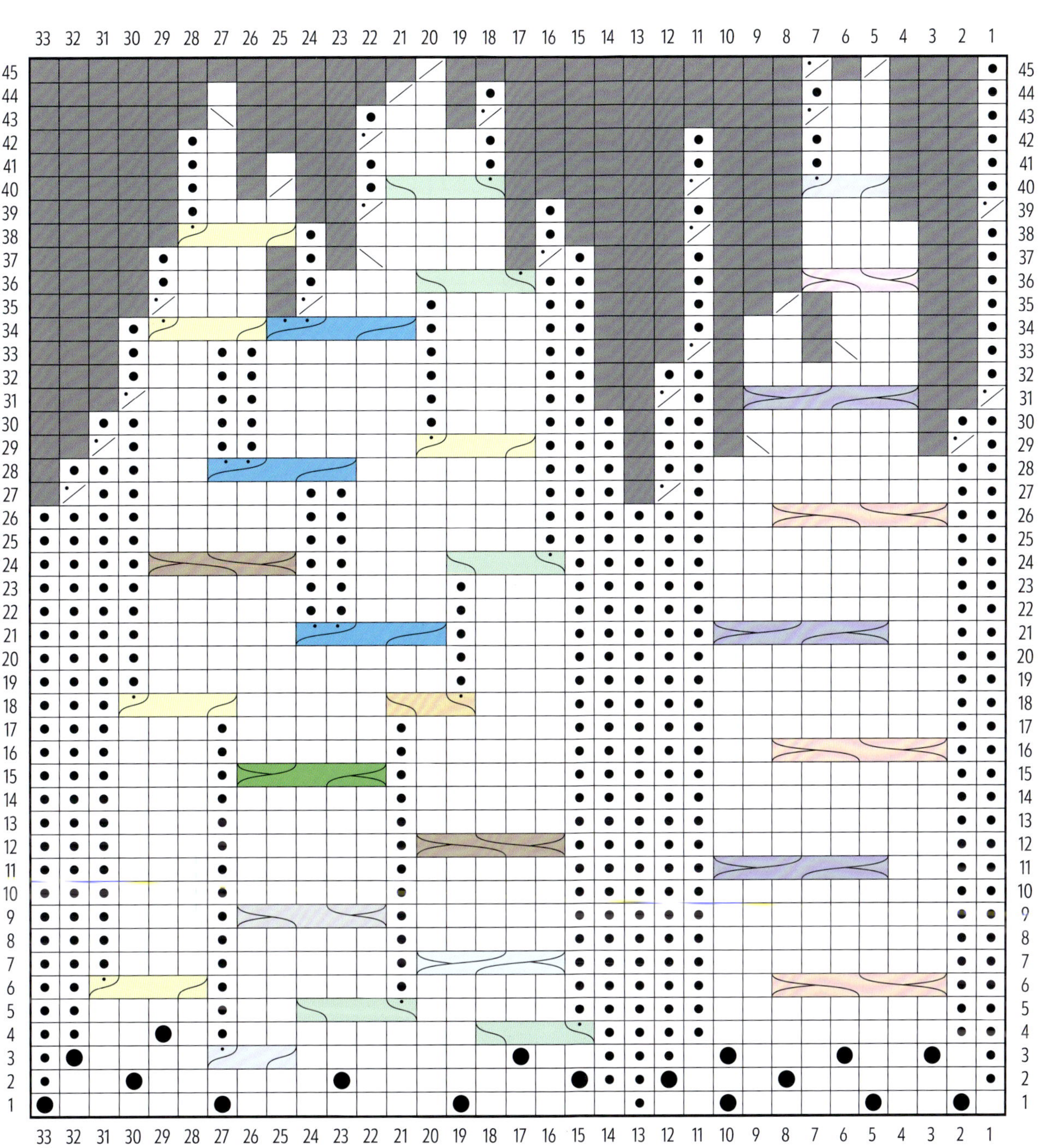

When you ask most folks what comes to mind when they think about Texas, cowboys (and the boots and hats that go with them) will likely be near the top of the list! In the early 1800s, cowboy boots were designed strictly for function. The leather was sturdy and protected the rider's calves, the stitching helped the leather keep its shape, the narrowed toe made it easier to slip the boot into stirrups, while the heel kept them from sliding out. Fast forward a couple hundred years and you'll find incredible (and often unexpected) artistry and craftsmanship in boots for the entire family. Today's cowboy boots might feature colorful patterns, embroidery, or even rhinestones and metallic stitching.

This design was inspired by the stitching patterns and worn leather of *classic* cowboy boots. The row of dark brown at the base of the ribbing represents the sole of the boot. If y'all want to personalize your boots a little, try using a different color for the leather. Pink, blue, black—the choice is yours!

SIZE

One size fits an average adult size head (approx. 19 in. / 48 cm – 22 in. / 56 cm)

Finished Circumference: approx. 20¼ in. / 51.5 cm.

YARN

Worsted weight yarn (#4) in three colors. Shown in:

A: Malabrigo Rios: Coco, not shown on chart. (5 g / 11 yd. / 10 m)

B: Aly Bee Workshop Merino Worsted: Cold Brew (50 g / 100 yd. / 91 m)

C: Malabrigo Rios: Ivory (33 g / 69 yd. / 63 m)

NEEDLES

- US size 5 / 3.75 mm, 16 in. / 40 cm circular knitting needles
- US size 7 / 4.5 mm, 16 in. / 40 cm circular knitting needles
- US size 7 / 4.5 mm, set of double-pointed needles (DPNs)
- (or size needed to obtain gauge)

Continued on next page

NOTIONS

3 stitch markers (two of one color and one of another color)

Tapestry needle for weaving in ends

GAUGE

With larger needles, approx. 9½ stitches = 2 in. / 5 cm in stranded stockinette stitch, blocked.

Note: If you already know you are a tight knitter (or just want a larger hat), go up one or two needle sizes for both the ribbing and the body of the hat.

With smaller circular needles and **color A**, cast on 96 stitches. Place single color marker and join in the round, being careful not to twist stitches.

Work (k1, p1) rib pattern for **1 or 2 rows**, depending on how thick you want the "sole" of your boots. I used one row. **Change to color B**, and continue to work (k1, p1) rib pattern until total ribbing measures approximately 1½ to 2 in. / 4 to 5 cm.

Switch to larger needles and work chart from right to left beginning on Row 1, bottom right corner. Chart repeats three times around the hat. Use remaining two stitch markers of another color to mark chart repeats.

Note: In order to avoid long "floats" (strands of yarn on the inside of the hat) and to help maintain your tension, do not carry a color more than three or four stitches without twisting the colors around each other in the back of work.

Switch to DPNs when work becomes too small for circular needles.

FINISHING

After chart is complete, cut yarn leaving a 10 in. / 25.5 cm tail. Using a tapestry needle, weave tail through remaining stitches and pull tightly to close circle. Pull tail to inside and weave in all ends.

Block as desired. See page 13 for my favorite hat blocking technique.

KEY

□ K
Knit

◩ K2tog
Knit 2 together

■ No Stitch
The "no stitch" squares represent the stitches that were lost due to decreases earlier in the round. *Do not skip a stitch*. Simply treat these squares as if they do not exist.

⧅ ssk
Slip, slip, knit: Slip 2 stitches knitwise, place stitches back on left needle, knit 2 tog through back loop

When you have a state that's famous for the Mighty 5 (the five beautiful national parks in Utah), it might leave some people wondering "What else is there?" The answer is: plenty! The signature red rock features of Utah abound in numerous state parks and national landmarks that rival the national parks in beauty and grandeur. The world-renowned land-speed racing site, Bonneville Salt Flats, has been attracting drivers hoping to break new speed records since the 1930s. The cultural impact of Native Americans, early pioneers, and Mormons is honored in historical sites, museums, and landmarks throughout the state. The state's art, culinary, and music scene thrives through galleries, concerts, and various special events, including the Utah Arts Festival and the world-famous Sundance Film Festival.

This design focuses on the simple beauty of the Utah state flower: the sego lily. These lovely flowers thrive in dry, sandy soil and pop up in unexpected places, making them a joy to spot in the wild. The plant's bulb served as a food source for Native Americans and early settlers.

SIZE

One size fits an average adult size head (approx. 19 in. / 48 cm – 22 in. / 56 cm)

Finished Circumference: approx. 20¼ in. / 51.5 cm.

YARN

Worsted weight yarn (#4) in four colors. Shown in:

- **A:** Malabrigo Rios: Ivy (25 g / 53 yd. / 48 m)
- **B:** Stunning String Studio Legacy Worsted: Oregon Trail (50 g / 108 yd. / 99 m)
- **C:** Aly Bee Workshop Merino Worsted: Sweet Cream (20 g / 40 yd. / 37 m)
- **D:** *Stunning String Studio Legacy Worsted: Sunkissed (10 g/ 21 yd./ 19 m)

*Used only in duplicate stitching

Approximately 3-5 yd / 2.75-4 m of purple/ burgundy yarn for the details on the flowers. I used Merino Worsted Boysenberry from Aly Bee Workshop.

Continued on next page

NEEDLES

- US size 5 / 3.75 mm, 16 in. / 40 cm circular knitting needles
- US size 7 / 4.5 mm, 16 in. / 40 cm circular knitting needles
- US size 7 / 4.5 mm, set of double-pointed needles (DPNs)
- (or size needed to obtain gauge)

NOTIONS

3 stitch markers (two of one color and one of another color)

Tapestry needle for weaving in ends and working duplicate stitches and embroidery

GAUGE

With larger needles, approx. 9½ stitches = 2 in. / 5 cm in stranded stockinette stitch, blocked.

Note: If you already know you are a tight knitter (or just want a larger hat), go up one or two needle sizes for both the ribbing and the body of the hat.

With smaller circular needles and color A, cast on 96 stitches. Place single color marker and join in the round, being careful not to twist stitches.

Work (k1, p1) rib pattern for approximately 1½ to 2 in. / 4 to 5 cm.

Switch to larger needles and work chart from right to left beginning on Row 1, bottom right corner. Chart repeats three times around the hat. Use remaining two stitch markers of another color to mark chart repeats.

Note: In order to avoid long "floats" (strands of yarn on the inside of the hat) and to help maintain your tension, do not carry a color more than three or four stitches without twisting the colors around each other in the back of work.

Switch to DPNs when work becomes too small for circular needles.

FINISHING

After chart is complete, cut yarn leaving a 10 in. / 25.5 cm tail. Using a tapestry needle, weave tail through remaining stitches and pull tightly to close circle. Pull tail to inside and weave in all ends.

Block as desired. See page 13 for my favorite hat blocking technique.

After all knitting and blocking is complete, work duplicate stitches where shown using a tapestry needle. With purple/ burgundy yarn, add details to flower centers using simple straight stitches. See photo for inspiration.

KEY

☐ K
Knit

D Dup
Work duplicate stitches after all knitting and blocking is complete.

⧄ K2tog
Knit 2 together

■ No Stitch
The "no stitch" squares represent the stitches that were lost due to decreases earlier in the round. *Do not skip a stitch.* Simply treat these squares as if they do not exist.

The varied climate zones in Washington range from semiarid in the east to lush rainforests in the west—and just about everything else in between. Agriculture, adventure tourism, lumber production, wineries, and manufacturing each thrive in perfect conditions. Even the foggy and overcast days that make Seattle one of the least sunny cities in the country also help create the spectacular forests that cover half of the state, earning it the nickname the Evergreen State. Whether the day is bright and sunny or drenched in rain, there's something about a forest that draws you in and invites you to stay awhile. With just four colors, this design embodies the beauty of a fog-covered forest on a dreary day.

Fun fact: Did you know that Washington has had more Sasquatch sightings than any other state? If you're a believer (even just a little), add a Sasquatch to this forest design using scraps of any brown yarn and a few simple stitches.

SIZE

One size fits an average adult size head (approx. 19 in. / 48 cm – 22 in. / 56 cm)

Finished Circumference: approx. 20¼ in. / 51.5 cm.

YARN

Worsted weight yarn (#4) in four colors. Shown in:

- **A:** Malabrigo Rios: VAA (40 g / 84 yd. / 77 m)
- **B:** Polka Dot Sheep Whitefish Worsted: Moose Meadow (20 g / 43 yd. / 39 m)
- **C:** Aly Bee Workshop Merino Worsted: Wasabi (20 g / 40 yd. / 37 m)
- **D:** Malabrigo Rios: Ivory (20 g / 42 yd. / 38 m)

Optional: A yard or so of any brown or tan yarn for an embroidered Sasquatch.

NEEDLES

- US size 5 / 3.75 mm, 16 in. / 40 cm circular knitting needles
- US size 7 / 4.5 mm, 16 in. / 40 cm circular knitting needles
- US size 7 / 4.5 mm, set of double-pointed needles (DPNs)
- (or size needed to obtain gauge)

Continued on next page

NOTIONS

3 stitch markers (two of one color and one of another color)

Tapestry needle for weaving in ends and working duplicate stitches and embroidery

GAUGE

With larger needles, approx. 9½ stitches = 2 in. / 5 cm in stranded stockinette stitch, blocked.

Note: If you already know you are a tight knitter (or just want a larger hat), go up one or two needle sizes for both the ribbing and the body of the hat.

With smaller circular needles and color A, cast on 96 stitches. Place single color marker and join in the round, being careful not to twist stitches.

Work (k1, p1) rib pattern for approximately 1½ to 2 in. / 4 to 5 cm.

Switch to larger needles and work chart from right to left beginning on Row 1, bottom right corner. Chart repeats three times around the hat. Use remaining two stitch markers of another color to mark chart repeats.

Note: The beauty of this design comes from the depth of the layers of trees created with 4 colors. If you prefer to knit with only 2 colors at a time (as I do), you will need to add quite a bit of duplicate stitches afterwards. If you are comfortable knitting with 3–4 colors at once, simply ignore the D symbols and knit in the colors shown.

Note: In order to avoid long "floats" (strands of yarn on the inside of the hat) and to help maintain your tension, do not carry a color more than three or four stitches without twisting the colors around each other in the back of work.

Switch to DPNs when work becomes too small for circular needles.

FINISHING

After chart is complete, cut yarn leaving a 10 in. / 25.5 cm tail. Using a tapestry needle, weave tail through remaining stitches and pull tightly to close circle. Pull tail to inside and weave in all ends.

Block as desired. See page 13 for my favorite hat blocking technique.

After all knitting and blocking is complete, work duplicate stitches where shown using a tapestry needle.

Optional: Add a little Sasquatch to your forest using straight stitches for the body and a French knot for the head. A yard or so of any color brown will work. See photo for inspiration.

KEY

☐ K
Knit

D Dup
Work duplicate stitches after all knitting and blocking is complete.

/ K2tog
Knit 2 together

■ No Stitch
The "no stitch" squares represent the stitches that were lost due to decreases earlier in the round. *Do not skip a stitch*. Simply treat these squares as if they do not exist.

	32	31	30	29	28	27	26	25	24	23	22	21	20	19	18	17	16	15	14	13	12	11	10	9	8	7	6	5	4	3	2	1	
45											/										/									/			45
44																																	44
43											/								/						/								43
42																																	42
41							/								/															/			41
40																																	40
39											/								/						/								39
38																																	38
37							/								/												/						37
36																																	36
35											/										/									/			35
34																																	34
33				/																				/									33
32																										D							32
31							/										/									D			/				31
30																									D	D	D						30
29		/											/						/							D							29
28																				D					D	D	D						28
27	D			/						D									D	D	D					D						/	27
26	D									D										D					D	D	D						26
25	D	D							D	D	D								D	D	D					D						D	25
24	D									D										D				D	D	D	D	D					24
23									D	D	D															D				D			23
22										D															D	D	D			D			22
21									D	D	D															D			D	D	D		21
20										D														D	D	D	D	D		D			20
19								D	D	D	D	D				D										D			D	D	D		19
18										D					D	D	D						D	D	D	D	D	D	D	D			18
17								D	D	D	D	D				D										D		D	D	D	D	D	17
16					D					D					D	D	D							D	D	D	D	D		D			16
15					D				D	D	D					D										D		D	D	D	D	D	15
14																																	14
13																																	13
12																																	12
11																																	11
10																																	10
9																																	9
8																																	8
7																																	7
6																																	6
5																																	5
4																																	4
3																																	3
2																																	2
1																																	1
	32	31	30	29	28	27	26	25	24	23	22	21	20	19	18	17	16	15	14	13	12	11	10	9	8	7	6	5	4	3	2	1	

Beneath this wide-open state filled with spectacular mountain ranges, jaw-dropping scenery, cowboys, and cattle ranches lie some of the most prolific fossil deposits in the country. Paleontology is so much a part of Wyoming's history that it has an official state dinosaur (triceratops) and state fossil (a fish). Fossilized frogs, turtles, fish, and insects reveal to scientists that much of Wyoming (at various periods in time) was covered in shallow seas and massive freshwater lakes. Dinosaurs roamed the area, too. The sedimentary layers of the seas trapped the remains of plant and animal life, creating the perfect environment for fossils to form. The seas and lakes eventually withdrew, revealing the rich deposits of marine and dinosaur fossils formed over millions of years. Once discovered, fossil dig sites attracted paleontologists and amateur fossil hunters from around the world. And still do!

In four earthy colors, create your own knitted version of fish and dragonfly fossils along with the ever-popular triceratops, surrounded by a fun pattern of stylized sedimentary layers.

SIZE

One size fits an average adult size head (approx. 19 in. / 48 cm – 22 in. / 56 cm)

Finished Circumference: approx. 20¼ in. / 51.5 cm.

YARN

Worsted weight yarn (#4) in four colors. Shown in:

- **A:** Aly Bee Workshop Merino Worsted: Cobweb (33 g/ 66 yd./ 60 m)
- **B:** Aly Bee Workshop Merino Worsted: Scarecrow (20 g / 40 yd. / 37 m)
- **C:** Dream in Color Classy: Rochambeau (25 g / 55 yd. / 50 m)
- **D:** Stunning String Studio Legacy Worsted: Desert Floor (20 g / 43 yd. / 39 m)

Continued on next page

NEEDLES

- US size 5 / 3.75 mm, 16 in. / 40 cm circular knitting needles
- US size 7 / 4.5 mm, 16 in. / 40 cm circular knitting needles
- US size 7 / 4.5 mm, set of double-pointed needles (DPNs)
- (or size needed to obtain gauge)

NOTIONS

3 stitch markers (two of one color and one of another color)

Tapestry needle for weaving in ends

GAUGE

With larger needles, approx. 9½ stitches = 2 in. / 5 cm in stranded stockinette stitch, blocked.

Note: If you already know you are a tight knitter (or just want a larger hat), go up one or two needle sizes for both the ribbing and the body of the hat.

With smaller circular needles and color A, cast on 96 stitches. Place single color marker and join in the round, being careful not to twist stitches.

Work (k2, p2) rib pattern for approximately 1½ to 2 in. / 4 to 5 cm.

Switch to larger needles and work chart from right to left beginning on Row 1, bottom right corner. Chart repeats three times around the hat. Use remaining two stitch markers of another color to mark chart repeats.

Switch to DPNs when work becomes too small for circular needles.

FINISHING

After chart is complete, cut yarn leaving a 10 in. / 25.5 cm tail. Using a tapestry needle, weave tail through remaining stitches and pull tightly to close circle. Pull tail to inside and weave in all ends.

Block as desired. See page 13 for my favorite hat blocking technique.

KEY

■ No Stitch
The "no stitch" squares represent the stitches that were lost due to decreases earlier in the round. *Do not skip a stitch.* Simply treat these squares as if they do not exist.

□ K
Knit

⧄ K2tog
Knit 2 together

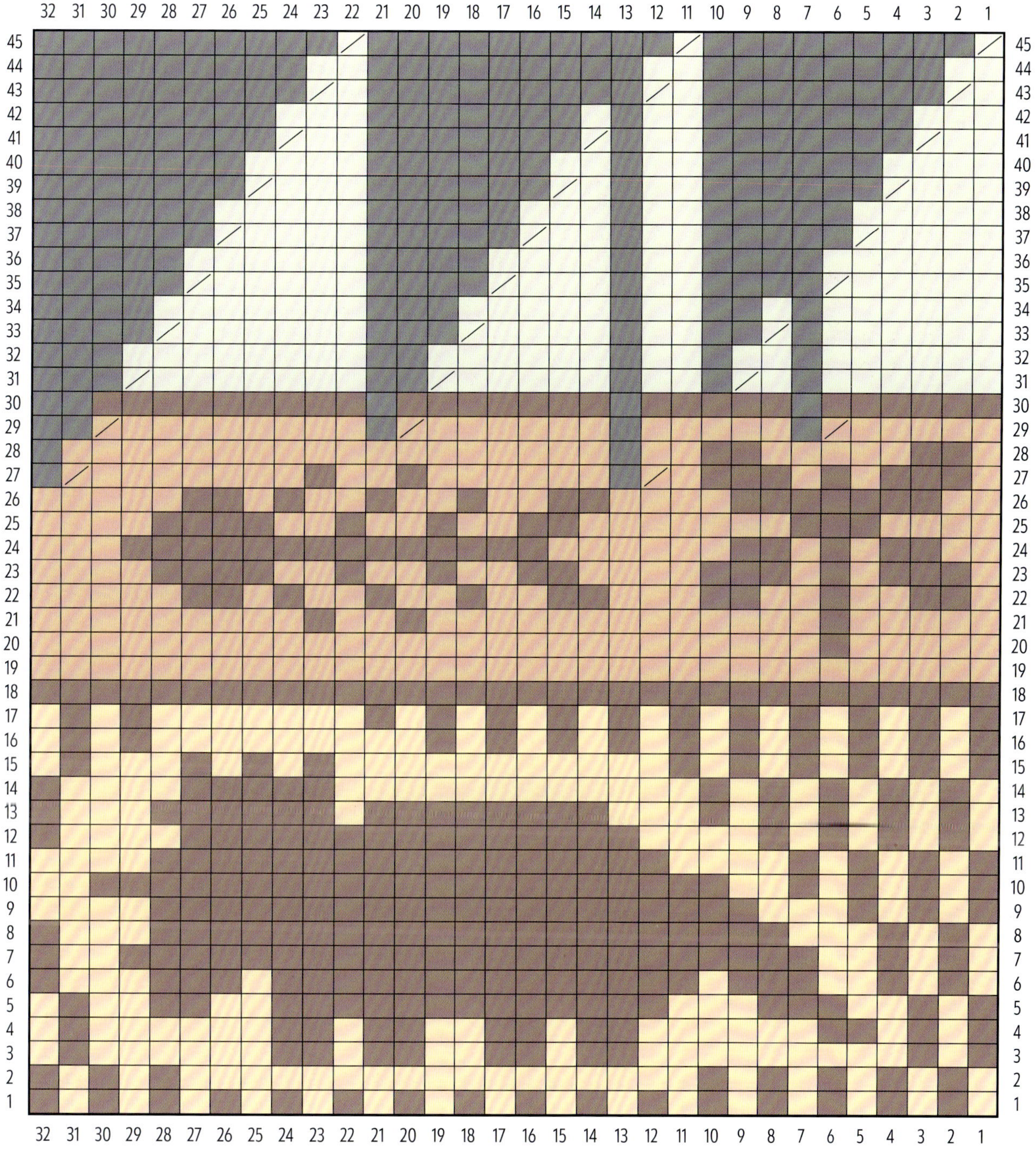

32 31 30 29 28 27 26 25 24 23 22 21 20 19 18 17 16 15 14 13 12 11 10 9 8 7 6 5 4 3 2 1

BEANIES IN THE WILD

Madelyn in Minnesota
Mary in Connecticut
Nona in Iowa
Lisa in Maryland
Gehrig in Tennessee
Dave in Georgia

RESOURCES

Yarn Kits & Beanie Labels
Nancy Bates Designs
nancybatesdesigns.com

Novelty Buttons & Charms
Car, turtle, and insect shaped buttons and lantern charms were all found through various sellers on Etsy

Yarn
Note: If you don't immediately see the colors that you need from the smaller indie dyers, be sure to send them a message.

Aly Bee Workshop
alybeeworkshop.com

Apple Fiber Studio
applefiberstudio.com

Berroco
berroco.com

Dragonfly Fibers and Canon Hand Dyes
canonhanddyes.com

Dream in Color Yarn
dreamincoloryarn.com

Ewe2Yarn
ewe2yarn.com

Fiber Seed Yarn Co.
thefiberseed.com

Malabrigo
malabrigoyarn.com

Peekaboo Yarns
etsy.com/shop/PeekabooYarns

Polka Dot Sheep
polkadotsheep.com

Schmutzerella Yarns
schmutzerellayarns.com

Seismic Yarn & Dyeworks
seismicyarn.com

Storyteller Stitchery
storytellerstitchery.com

Stunning String Studio
stunningstring.com

INDEX OF PROJECTS

TECHNIQUES GLOSSARY

APPLYING/PLACING BEADS

Crochet Hook Method

Using a crochet or bead hook appropriate for the size of bead being used, insert the hook through the bead and leave the bead on the hook. With the crochet hook, pick up the loop of the stitch over which you want to place the bead and let it drop off your knitting needle. Pull this loop through the bead, place the loop back onto the left-hand needle, and remove the crochet hook. Knit this stitch in pattern to secure the bead.

Stringing Method

Before any knitting begins, using a tapestry needle or sewing needle appropriate for the size of bead being used, thread the needle with the tail of yarn for your project. Place all of the beads you plan to use onto the needle, then pull them down the shaft of the needle and onto the working yarn. Move the beads down the yarn an appropriate length to allow you to cast on. Continue to move the beads down the yarn as you knit.

*To apply the bead, knit to your desired bead location. Then move the working yarn to the front of the work between the needles. Slide 1 bead along the working yarn until it is adjacent to the needle, in front of the work.

Slip the next stitch purlwise with the working yarn in front and slide the bead into place so that it nestles into the V of the slipped stitch.

Return the working yarn to the back between the needles and continue working in pattern.

Repeat from * until all beads are placed.

CAST ONS

Long Tail Cast On

Make a slipknot with the yarn, leaving a tail long enough to cast on the required number of stitches (usually about 1 in. / 2.5 cm per stitch), and place the slipknot onto the needle. Holding the needle in your right hand, clasp both strands for the cast on in the lower three fingers of your left hand with the long tail over your thumb and the end coming from the ball over your index finger.

*Spread your thumb and index finger apart to form a V. Insert the needle tip up between the two strands on your thumb. Bring the needle tip over the top of the first strand around your index finger, then down to draw a loop between the strands on your thumb. Remove your

thumb and tighten the stitch on the needle—1 stitch cast on. Place your thumb and index finger between the strands of yarn again.

Repeat from * until the required number of stitches has been cast on.

DUPLICATE STITCH

Duplicate stitch is a way of adding sections of color to a knitted piece without having to work stranded knitting or intarsia. The technique covers each stitch completely. Large areas can become thick and stiff, so it's best used in small areas.

With the color to be stitched threaded into a tapestry needle, insert the needle from wrong side to right side in the stitch below the first stitch to be covered.

*Insert the tapestry needle under both legs of the stitch in the row above the stitch to be covered and pull the yarn through, being careful not to pull the yarn too tightly. Insert the needle back into the same spot where you initially brought it to the right side, and pull the yarn through to completely cover the first stitch. Bring the needle up through the stitch below the next stitch to be covered.

Repeat from * to continue covering stitches.

FRENCH KNOT

An embroidery method used to embellish your work by creating a decorative knot that is raised from the working surface.

Thread a tapestry needle with a length of yarn approximately 12 in. / 30.5 cm long (for multiple knots; less length for a single knot).

Push the tapestry needle through the work from the wrong side to the right side (or back to front), leaving 2 in. /5 cm of tail on the wrong side of the work for weaving in.

Holding the embroidery needle close to the surface of the work, wrap the working yarn around the tapestry needle one or two times, depending on desired size of knot.

Using your pointer finger, hold the wraps against the tapestry needle and push the needle back through the work from the right side to the wrong side (or front to back) beside/near the original location (not into the same location to avoid the knot pulling through the work) and pull the yarn through the knot. Do not pull too snugly to avoid flattening the knot.

MODEL AND PHOTOGRAPHY CREDITS

Thanks to all of the models who appear in this book:

Allyson Baily
14,16, 24, 62

Caitlin Bates
36, 116, 128, 132, 218

Nancy Bates
14, 32, 48, 124, 160, 174, 190

Natalie Bates
20, 40, 160, 162, 186, 214

Scott Bates
70, 120, 140, 144

Kimberly Brewer
102, 160, 198

Delaney Brewer
110

Kayli Brewer
86

Yvonne Dobie
82

Linda Durant Flores
110

Arnold González
8, 202

Verónica A. González
2, 14, 28, 152

Robert Herrera
170

Ryan Jordan
90

Diane Kuehl
194

Jesse Levotch
148

Joe Machan
60

Richard Machan
110, 136, 232

Staci Machan
206, 232

Laura Slobojan Moore
52

Jason Rodriguez
60, 66, 106, 182, 228

Sally Schultzman
44

Susan Stearns
11

Alyson Sutton
56, 74, 94, 156, 178, 210

Neel Sutton
60, 78, 98

Brenda Thibert
112

Yvette
166

All beanie model photography courtesy the Bates Family.
All location images courtesy Shutterstock, except for the following:
page 71—Jason Gulley; page 91—Skip Pudney.

ACKNOWLEDGMENTS

So much of my gratitude regarding this project goes to about two hundred people I've never met. It's true! To everyone who enthusiastically answered my call on social media and in person to "Tell me what you love about your home state," I can't thank you enough. As the responses rolled in, the state pride I felt from around the country was infectious, and my inspiration soared. Your input brought an authenticity to the designs that wouldn't have been possible through research and my personal experience alone. Thank you from the bottom of my heart!

To my amazing test knitters, tech editors, and friends Sally Schultzman and Nona Davenport, a *million* thanks for making sure the ideas in my head could easily be shared with others. The projects may be small, but the love that went into each and every one of them was enormous—and I felt it.

I am thrilled and incredibly thankful that I was able to include my eight siblings in this book from being sounding boards for ideas to models on the pages. I'm so grateful to all of you and to Kim for being a most excellent stylist!

My appreciation for the endless love and encouragement from my husband, Scott, and daughters, Natalie, Caitlin, and Alyson (and son-in-law Neel), can't be expressed enough. When I say, "I couldn't have done it without you," I mean it. From your design and color input and photo-editing skills to your talent in front of and behind the camera, I will forever be amazed and grateful.

Always, to my editors, Karyn and Jon, and publisher, Roger, thank you for believing in me.

Lastly, to the knitters of my hats around the country and around the world, thank you for joining me on this incredible journey. Much love to all of you!

ABOUT THE AUTHOR

Nancy's first exposure to traveling the fifty states came on a cross-country road trip (California to Ontario, Canada) when she was seven years old—with the entire family of eleven loaded into the green Ford Country Squire and an equal number of suitcases strapped to the roof. What an adventure! Even at a young age, that trip lit a spark that eventually led to a life-long passion for exploring places beyond her home state. Today she travels with her husband (and three daughters whenever possible) to explore national parks, experience other seasons and landscapes, and simply enjoy and appreciate what the rest of the United States has to offer. And there's *a LOT* to explore!

Outside of knitting, Nancy's passions include sewing, crochet, embroidery, painting, cross-stitch, outdoor cooking, and hiking. Her favorite pastime of all is spending time with her growing family and eight siblings, including the annual Sister Week, a week-long gathering of all seven sisters.

Also the author of *Knitting the National Parks* and *Knitting California*, Nancy can be found on Instagram and Facebook and teaching workshops and meeting fellow knitters and adventurers around the country. Her favorite part of this design journey has been hearing stories and seeing photos of all the places her beanies (and the passionate knitters behind them) have been.

weldon**owen**
an imprint of Insight Editions
P.O. Box 3088
San Rafael, CA 94912
www.weldonowen.com

CEO Raoul Goff
SVP Group Publisher Jeff McLaughlin
VP Publisher Roger Shaw
Executive Editor Karyn Gerhard
Editorial Assistant Jon Ellis
Managing Editor Michelle Hope
VP Creative Chrissy Kwasnik
Art Director Megan Sinead Bingham
Production Design Jean Hwang
VP Manufacturing Alix Nicholaeff
Production Manager Joshua Smith
Strategic Production Planner Lina s Palma-Temena

Weldon Owen would also like to thank Meaghan Schmaltz, Jessica Easto, and Carla Kipen for their work on this project.

ISBN: 979-8-88674-275-6

Manufactured in China by Insight Editions
10 9 8 7 6 5 4 3 2 1

Insight Editions, in association with Roots of Peace, will plant two trees for each tree used in the manufacturing of this book. Roots of Peace is an internationally renowned humanitarian organization dedicated to eradicating land mines worldwide and converting war-torn lands into productive farms and wildlife habitats. Roots of Peace will plant two million fruit and nut trees in Afghanistan and provide farmers there with the skills and support necessary for sustainable land use.